FROM PROPHECY TO CHARITY
How to Help the Poor

FROM PROPHECY TO CHARITY
How to Help the Poor

Lawrence M. Mead

AEI Press
Publisher for the American Enterprise Institute
Washington, D.C.

Distributed by arrangement with the National Book Network
15200 NBN Way, Blue Ridge Summit, PA 17214
To order call toll free 1-800-462-6420 or 1-717-794-3800.

For all other inquiries please contact AEI Press, 1150 17th Street,
N.W., Washington, D.C. 20036 or call 1-800-862-5801.

Mead, Lawrence M.
  From prophecy to charity : how to help the
poor / Lawrence M. Mead.
    p. cm.
  Includes bibliographical references.
  ISBN-13: 978-0-8447-4380-6 (pbk.)
  ISBN-10: 0-8447-4380-1 (pbk.)
  ISBN-13: 978-0-8447-4381-3 (ebook)
  ISBN-10: 0-8447-4381-X (ebook)
  1. Public welfare—United States. 2. Poor—United States.
  3. Poverty—United States. I. Title.
  HV95.M347 2011
  362.5'5—dc23

CONTENTS

LIST OF TABLES

LIST OF ACRONYMS

AFDC	Aid to Families with Dependent Children
EITC	Earned Income Tax Credit
MRDC	Manpower Demonstration Research Corporation
NCLB	No Child Left Behind
PRWORA	Personal Responsibility and Work Opportunity Reconciliation Act, 1996
SNAP	Supplemental Nutrition Assistance Program
TANF	Temporary Assistance for Needy Families

ACKNOWLEDGMENTS

I express appreciation to the American Enterprise Institute for commissioning this study and for the useful comments their editors and reviewers have made. However, responsibility for the final product is entirely mine.

INTRODUCTION

How should America respond to the presence of poor people in our midst? As the richest country on earth, the United States has great capacity to help the poor, and most Americans think we have a moral obligation to do so. Helping the poor is an important responsibility of government and of individuals and private organizations as well.

How best to help the poor, however, is not as clear as it may seem. Opinion leaders sometimes suggest we should simply spend more on the needy, giving them more benefits and services than they receive now. In this view, recent conservative administrations in Washington have unduly cut back our commitments. But our responsibility, I will argue, is not simply to spend more or less on the problem. Rather, it is to do what the poor most deeply require. Recent conservative policies are more effective than what came before, and it would be a mistake to abandon them.

The difficulty is that poverty involves more than low income. To defeat it does require spending money, but it also entails getting more of the needy to help themselves. The adult poor must work as other people do. Poor children must get through school and avoid trouble with the law and unwed pregnancy if they are to get ahead in life. Progress against poverty, then, requires programs with the capacity to redirect lives, not just transfer resources. Government has had some success in developing programs like this in recent years. Our best course is to continue down this road.

Ordinary Americans have practical views about poverty. They combine an earnest desire to help with an insistence that the poor help themselves. Political leaders, activists, and experts are much more polarized. Some have contended that the poor are entitled to aid regardless of lifestyle or, alternatively, that they should get nothing at all from government. Wiser views come from our religious traditions. In the Bible, God commands serious attention to the poor, but the emphasis is not on abstractions such as rights, freedom, or equality but on restoring community. That requires that there be right relationships among people within society and also between them and God. To that end, we must be generous toward the poor, but we should also expect good behavior from them.

A LOOK AHEAD

In the pages that follow, I describe America's poverty problem, various critical perspectives about it, and recent policy developments. I also discuss some broader issues. All these dimensions help us understand how best to respond to poverty today.

Chapter 1 discusses what poverty means, how government measures it, and who the poor are in America. In the public mind, poverty has an economic and a behavioral dimension. The poor are those who have unusually low income for the society *and* who often have problems coping with life. The government's measurement of poverty ignores the behavioral dimension, yet it cannot be avoided. The politics of poverty has reflected the public's will both to help the poor and expect more self-reliance. That dual emphasis is also seen in the programs against poverty that government already has. Although some think America should give more to the poor, as Europe does, Europe has lately followed America's lead in requiring work of many people living on benefits. That is because overcoming poverty cannot be imagined unless poor adults work more consistently than they have.

Chapter 2 addresses the crucial question of causes. How can it be that people are poor in the richest society on earth? Poverty tends to arise in the first place because poor parents have children outside marriage and then do not work regularly to support them. Thus, to explain poverty chiefly means explaining nonmarriage and nonwork. Those patterns, I will argue, cannot generally be traced to barriers to opportunity in the society, as many suppose. Culture and a failure to enforce norms such as work are more important. The history of antipoverty policy confirms this.

Chapter 3 takes up critical perspectives. How should we react to poverty as it is and to America's existing policies? Secular ideologies tend to run to extremes. A rights tradition says that the poor should simply be given more benefits without expectations, while a libertarian tradition denies them any claim on government at all. Both views have clear limitations. Our religious traditions suggest a different and wiser perspective. The Bible makes helping the poor a priority, but the emphasis is not on rights or economics but on rebuilding community. To that end, the poor must receive aid, but they must also fulfill community norms about work and family life. I also consider two influential versions of a Christian perspective—Catholic social teaching and the new social gospel—that, in my view, stray from the biblical tradition.

Chapter 4 describes the great watershed in recent social policy known as welfare reform. "Welfare" mainly means cash aid to needy families. Welfare families are mostly female headed, meaning that the mother heads the family and the father is absent. In the 1990s, after decades of controversy, the federal government radically reformed family welfare to require most welfare mothers to work as a condition of aid. Reform was a test of competing views about the causes of poverty and also the critical responses to poverty. Most experts opposed reform, believing that few poor could work, given the barriers they faced. But most welfare mothers successfully left the rolls for jobs, with most of the leavers emerging better off. That confirmed the view I have suggested, that whether the poor work mainly reflects whether they are expected to, not the extent of opportunity.

Most church organizations opposed reform, believing it was unjust. But the popularity of reform, as well as its success, has forced some reconsideration. The reformed welfare system, combining more generous support with clearer work expectations, is in fact closer to the biblical vision than what came before.

Chapter 5 suggests the way forward. Alongside the reformed welfare system, other social programs have appeared with a paternalist character. These not only aid the poor in various ways but also seek to redirect lifestyle. We need effective work programs to serve nonworking men as well as welfare mothers, and we need more authoritative schools that set clear standards for poor students. Religious believers and faith-based organizations can make important contributions to developing such programs. The door is open for renewed progress against poverty.

Chapter 6 considers two larger issues that shed light on our poverty struggle. First, how should we respond to poverty beyond our shores? Destitution in many developing countries is far worse than in America, and its causes seem very different. Yet here too, it turns out, the poor themselves must take more initiative than they usually have. The obligation to overcome poverty cannot rest only on the rich. The second question is how we should reason about poverty in the most general terms. Religious critics of our current policies tend to adopt the prophetic voice—to speak of justice and to judge society unilaterally in God's name. Under today's conditions, I argue, they should rather speak of charity and adopt a more modest and collaborative style.

1

POVERTY, POLITICS, AND PROGRAMS

The baseline for any response to poverty must be basic facts about the problem. In this chapter I describe what we mean by poverty, how government measures it, and who is poor in America. I also summarize how the public reacts to poverty, which is the basis of the politics of poverty. I describe the social programs we already have to ameliorate poverty. Government does more to help the poor than many people realize, but these programs generally respect the distinctions the public draws between the "deserving" and "undeserving."

WHAT IS POVERTY?

Poverty would be a simple problem if it only meant economic need. Sometimes it does. Children, the elderly and disabled, and families in the grip of natural disasters—all can be made destitute by forces beyond their control. But in an affluent society like ours, poverty is not usually forced on people for very long by conditions. Typically it has a behavioral dimension as well: The poor may suffer from low wages or health problems, for example, but most have become poor, at least in part, due to not working, having children outside marriage, abusing drugs, or breaking the law. This is particularly true for people who remain poor for more than a year or two.

Ordinary Americans understand this. Typically, the public regards people as poor when they have unusually low income for the society, *and* when they also exhibit some loss of control over their lives. The involvement of lifestyle is the main reason why helping the poor is difficult. Typically, it is not enough just to give the needy more resources. Something must also be done to change behavior, to get those we help to live more constructive lives.

The discourse that surrounds poverty in Washington, however, is overwhelmingly economic, that is, all about income and benefit levels, incentives, and "human capital." Poverty is treated as a condition that is widespread and involuntary. The behavioral side of the problem is usually ignored. But realism requires that it be acknowledged.

THE EXACT POVERTY LINE VARIES WITH FAMILY SIZE. IN 2009, IT WAS $17,285 FOR A FAMILY OF THREE, INCLUDING TWO CHILDREN. THIS FIGURE WAS MUCH BELOW THE TYPICAL HOUSEHOLD INCOME IN THAT YEAR, WHICH WAS $49,777.[2]

Source: U.S. Department of Commerce, Bureau of the Census.

The Poverty Measure. The way the federal government measures poverty ignores lifestyle entirely. Back in the early 1960s, government economists defined poverty as having an income less than three times the cost of a minimal food budget. At that time the typical family spent about a third of its income on food. Families with income under this threshold were defined as poor.

Since then, the poverty line has been adjusted upward to account for inflation but not for the growth in real incomes. Originally, the line was about half the typical family's income after taxes; today it is about a third.[1]

The exact poverty line varies with family size. In 2009, it was $17,285 for a family of three, including two children. This figure was much below the typical household income in that year, which was $49,777.[2] On the other hand, it was vastly above the income of less than $2 a day that the World Bank uses to calculate poverty in developing countries. *Very* few if any of the American poor are destitute by that standard.

The government also overestimates how many people are poor by its standard. Officially, 14.3 percent of Americans were poor in 2009, up from 13.2 percent the previous year. But the official measure considers only cash income measured on a pretax basis. This excludes some benefits that many poor families receive in kind rather than in cash, such as food stamps, health care, and public housing. These programs provide the poor with food and other necessities without giving them money that they can spend as they wish. The measure also excludes the Earned Income Tax Credit (EITC), an important wage subsidy that low-income workers receive after taxes. The rules also overstate income in some ways, for instance by not deducting the expenses that people incur in order to work, such as for child care. But on balance, the official definition exaggerates the extent of poverty.

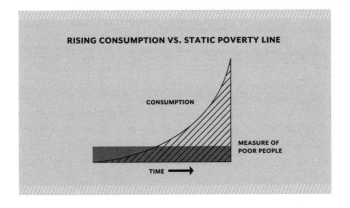

A more serious problem is that the official measure is stated in terms of income. To measure consumption would be a better gauge of living standards. To do that suggests that actual hardship is well below the official poverty rate. In surveys, low-income families report consuming at levels costing nearly twice the income they report, and this discrepancy has grown over time. This is partly because people understate their actual income, often innocently. The official poverty level has changed only a few points since 1970, yet consumption has risen dramatically for rich and poor alike.[3] Today, most households that the government calls poor own amenities such as microwave ovens and VCRs that did not exist decades ago. In 1995–97, 41 percent of poor households owned their own homes, and 70 percent owned a car or truck.[4] The poor do have much less than

TABLE 1. POVERTY IN THE UNITED STATES, 2009

	NO. IN GROUP *in millions*	NO. OF POOR *in millions*	PERCENT OF GROUP POOR	PERCENT OF PEOPLE FROM THIS GROUP	PERCENT OF POOR FROM THIS GROUP
All persons	304	44	14.3	100	100
Male	149	19	13.0	49	45
Female	155	24	15.6	51	55
White alone [a]	242	30	12.3	80	68
Black alone	39	10	25.8	13	23
Hispanic	49	12	25.3	16	28
Asian alone	14	2	12.5	5	4
Under age 18	75	15	20.7	25	35
Aged 18 to 64	191	25	12.9	63	57
Aged 65 & over	39	3	8.9	13	8
In metro areas	256	36	13.9	84	82
Central cities	98	18	18.7	32	42
Suburbs	158	17	11.0	52	40
In nonmetro areas	48	8	16.6	16	18
Northeast	55	7	12.2	18	15
Midwest	66	9	13.3	22	20
South	112	18	15.7	37	40
West	71	11	14.8	23	24
In families [b]	249	31	12.5	82	72
Two-parent [c]	188	14	7.2	62	31
Female-headed	45	15	32.5	15	34
Unrelated Individuals	53	12	22.0	17	27
On means-tested aid	92	32	34.3	30	72
On cash aid	20	8	41.5	6	19
On food stamps	34	20	58.1	11	46

Source: U.S. Bureau of the Census, March 2010 Annual Social and Economic Supplement, tables 1–2, 26, 41.
Note: Some figures do not add due to rounding. a. Races add to more than total because of double counting (Hispanics may be of any race), b. Families and unrelated individuals add to less than total because unrelated subfamilies are omitted, c. Family types add to less than total because male-headed single parent families are omitted.

the middle class, but they are often less needy than the label "poverty" suggests.

WHO ARE THE POOR?

The official poverty estimates suggest that poverty is widespread. Table 1 shows the official poverty rate for various groups in the society in 2009. It also shows the size of each group and the shares of the population and the poor drawn from each of them. In a given year, many different people are poor for different reasons. Poverty can arise from any disruption in normal income, due perhaps to unemployment, bad health, or the breakup of a marriage. By one estimate, over twenty-five years, as much as half of the American population will be poor for at least a year.[5]

But the official figures capture poverty only in a single year. The poverty that concerns most citizens and policymakers lasts longer than this. The official measure is based on a fresh survey annually, so it does not show whether the people poor in one year are also poor in other years. Longitudinal surveys that follow the same people over time suggest that the rate of long-term poverty is about half the official rate, or 6 to 7 percent.[6] The demographics of short- and long-term poverty are quite different. In table 1, the one-year poor look much like the general population. Two-thirds of them are white. Racial minorities and people living in female headed families are somewhat overrepresented. For the long-term poor, however, the latter groups dominate.

Among people poor for at least eight years out of ten, 44 percent live in female-headed families, and 62 percent are black. A similar contrast holds for short-term versus long-term welfare recipients.[7]

Long-term poverty or welfare dependency typically occurs because of the behavioral side of poverty that official statistics ignore. Serious poverty among the working-aged population is usually linked to unwed childbearing and failure to work. I will use the term "serious poverty" to connote people who are poor for at least two years at a stretch. That is the group I am thinking of when I reason below about the causes of and cures for poverty.

An important subgroup of poor is people on welfare, meaning benefits that are means tested, or given conditional on low income. According to table 1, in 2009 means-tested aid went to 72 percent of the poor and 30 percent of the population. Temporary Assistance for Needy Families (TANF), the program created by welfare reform, currently serves about 4.5 million people, but—under the name Aid to Families with Dependent Children (AFDC)—it was formerly much larger. TANF recipients mostly live in female-headed families, mostly with one or two children. In 2006, 38 percent the adult recipients were white, 36 percent black, and 21 percent Hispanic.[8]

THE POLITICS OF POVERTY

Advocates for the poor suggest that the public ignores

poverty problems. Polls show rather that Americans are conflicted. On the one hand, they are distressed by poverty. Knowing the wealth of the society, they do not understand why some people subsist on welfare for long periods or are seen begging on the streets. They want something done about this, and they criticize politicians who appear indifferent. Even under a conservative president like Ronald Reagan, popular support for generous antipoverty efforts remained strong.[9]

But at the same time, the public is upset by the behavioral side of poverty. Americans would prefer to help the needy who are poor for reasons beyond their control. They are offended by people who appear "undeserving," meaning those who seem to have made themselves poor, above all by not working. In surveys, the idea of helping needy families and children is popular, but "welfare" is unpopular, even though it may seem to mean the same thing. That is apparently because "welfare" connotes the most unpopular and permissive form of aid, where cash is given to people without expectations about behavior, above all about working.

To Americans, employment is the great emblem of deservingness. If the needy are working—or, alternatively, if they are clearly not able to work—people are much less conflicted about helping them. While the voters will also help the jobless but employable poor, they want to see clear evidence that the program is moving them toward work. Above all, the public seeks to turn poor adults into workers. The motivation is not to save money, although putting the poor to work can do that. Rather, working is seen as good in itself, a badge of citizenship, the capacity that especially integrates a person into society. To get people working, the public is willing to spend *more* than it does on the nonworking poor, as welfare reform showed. Although the public is also concerned about unwed pregnancy among the poor, it is currently much more tolerant of this than nonwork.[10]

A common academic view is that liberals are those who want to help the poor and conservatives are those who do not. Poverty does tend to polarize leadership groups, with those on the left demanding more aid and those on the right resisting. Ordinary Americans, however, are more inwardly divided. Left and right, they express sympathy toward people in difficulties, but they also demand that the poor do more to help themselves. Mass opinion about poverty and welfare is also little affected by which ideology or party is in power.

Another common interpretation is that ambivalence toward the poor is racist. Because most of the seriously poor are nonwhite, perhaps that is why white Americans often resist helping them. Welfare can seem unpopular because whites associate it with blacks, whom they view as undeserving.[11] The trouble with this view, however, is that blacks share whites' aversion to traditional welfare; they also want the recipients to do more to help themselves.[12] It is implausible that whites should be this hostile to blacks when most of them have abandoned racist beliefs in black inferiority and when government does many things to promote black advancement.[13] Debates about poverty and welfare in Washington or state capitals make little overt reference to race. That is probably because, although minorities are overrepresented among the poor, plenty of people of every race and ethnic group are involved.

A further interpretation of public attitudes is that the poverty or welfare problem is invented by politicians. Supposedly, leaders paint the needy or dependent as undeserving in order to justify hostile policies toward them or deflect attention from other problems that affect mainstream America, such as economic inequality.[14] However, there is little overt talk of deservingness in congressional debates on poverty.[15] And it is implausible to suggest that poverty and welfare are not real problems. Government has struggled with them for decades. The voters have enough contact with the poor to form their own opinions, and these must be taken seriously.

As these interpretations suggest, the most important division about poverty is not within the public but between it and the expert class that interprets poverty and welfare. In my experience, most academics and foundation officials who deal with these issues, as well as many journalists, are more liberal about them than average Americans. Above all, they are less conflicted. Most of them simply want more spent on the poor, and they deprecate letting concerns about deservingness stand in the way. Many believe in entitlement, the idea that the needy should qualify for aid simply by having low income, with no questions asked about lifestyle. That was the principle that welfare reform rejected.

WHAT GOVERNMENT DOES

From the criticisms made by experts and advocates, one might think that the poor are ignored in Washington. Actually, the nation already does a great deal to help them. Although public debate about poverty tends to be impersonal and ignore behavior, the benefits we provide reflect the public attitudes just surveyed. Whether the government helps people, and how much, depends critically on whether the recipients have a work connection. Programs are most generous toward those who have worked for what they get or who are clearly unable to work.

Social Insurance. Social Security provides pensions to the elderly and disabled, and Medicare provides health coverage for the same groups. These programs are huge, each serving around fifty million people. Social Security cost $701 billion and Medicare $447 billion in 2010— by far the costliest of all federal programs.[16] Costs will grow still further as the baby boom generation retires in coming years. How to reform these programs so that they do not bankrupt the government is a major issue.

Yet the programs are formidably popular. That is because they are based on the principle of social insurance. Beneficiaries contribute to funding them by paying Social Security taxes on their wages while they are employed. Thus, when they retire they can claim to have earned their benefits and do not feel dependent on the government. That is so even though, under current rules, the benefits they receive are actually far greater than could be financed by their payroll contributions alone.

Unemployment insurance is a third social insurance program. Here the employer pays payroll taxes on behalf of workers while they are employed. Then, if they lose their jobs through no fault of their own, they receive a benefit worth about half their previous earnings. Benefits usually last for six months, but Congress extends the time during recessions; currently, benefits can last nearly two years. Unemployment insurance, however, does not cover intermittent workers. To qualify you must have worked about half the time in the last year, and you must have earned some minimum amount, the details varying by state. Due to these rules, less than half of workers who become jobless actually receive this benefit.

The government also provides generous pension and health benefits to veterans of the military, and states provide compensation to workers who are injured on the job. These benefits, too, are based on an idea of prior contribution. People get them not mainly because they are needy but because they have earlier served the society, whether in uniform or on the job.

Welfare. Welfare means programs that are means tested, as opposed to social insurance, which is not. Recipients qualify for welfare initially because they have low income. Welfare is more controversial than social insurance primarily because its recipients usually have not been regularly employed. Thus, their deservingness is less clear. These programs cost much less than Social Security or Medicare, yet they are far less popular.

As noted earlier, the public is most accepting when welfare recipients are either working currently or clearly cannot work. Our largest welfare program is the Earned Income Tax Credit, a subsidy for low-paid workers that raises the earnings of parents with children by as much as 40 percent. EITC served twenty-five million taxpayers at a cost of $51 billion in 2008, yet it is popular precisely because benefits are conditioned on earnings.[17] On the other hand, Supplemental Security Income is also popular because it pays cash aid to aged, blind, or disabled people, whom we do not expect to work. This program served more than seven million people at a cost of $47 billion in 2010.[18]

Welfare for groups that are neither working nor unemployable is the most controversial exactly because they appear less deserving. One way government minimizes these concerns is by giving much of its aid in kind. Food stamps (now called the Supplemental Nutrition Assistance Program, or SNAP) helps families pay for groceries, while Medicaid provides health care to low-income families, and housing subsidies help many families afford shelter. Because these benefits can be used only for these purposes, concern about how recipients might spend them is muted.

TANF, which supports needy female-headed families, is the most controversial program because it unites all grounds for suspicion. Its cost is relatively small, around $28 billion in federal and state funds in 2006,[19] but the money goes to support families where most of the children are born outside marriage. Most of the adult recipients are employable, yet only a minority are working. Aid is also given in cash. These features aroused repeated struggles to reform the program, as I describe below.

Other Programs. The federal government also funds a plethora of smaller programs targeted to low-income individuals and families. Advocates believe these benefits do much to assuage poverty and seek more funding for them. The hard evidence suggests rather that the programs achieve less than claimed, either because the needs they address are already met or because they cannot produce the changes in lifestyle that are ultimately needed to overcome poverty.

The federal government funds child care for lower-income families on a large scale. Much of it is targeted to low-income mothers in an effort to get them to work and avoid welfare. Advocates think that current programs are insufficient or of low quality. They seek a national child care system that would cover all children, on the model of France or Sweden. However, most mothers needing care buy it from the private sector and are satisfied. There is no need for a national system. In their enthusiasm for larger government, advocates often misread what average Americans want.[20]

The government also subsidizes public education, even though this is largely a state and local function. Nothing appeals to Americans more than the idea of the poor getting ahead by succeeding in school, but the record of these programs is disappointing. Head Start is an early childhood education program that is supposed to prepare poor children for school, but evaluations suggest that it has little effect. Some experimental early childhood programs have done better, but few think that they could be generalized to the population and have the same impact. Washington also subsidizes the public schools and postsecondary education, but here too there is little evidence of positive impact. To try to improve results, the Bush administration recast federal school aid as No Child Left behind (NCLB) in 2002. Schools receiving the funds had to meet performance standards in an effort to hold them more accountable.

There are also federal training programs designed to help low-skilled youth and older workers improve their skills and wages after they have left school. These programs too have generally evaluated poorly. Clients who go through them emerge little better off than before. That is partly because the older programs are voluntary, with no power to require their clients to work. Some newer programs, as I note below, are more directive. These tell their clients more firmly what they must do to work and get ahead, and these evaluate better.

Do We Do Enough? Most academics think the American welfare state is simply too small. By certain measures, we have relatively more poor than other rich countries because we give them less. The difference in poverty is not great if need is measured by an absolute income threshold, as in the official poverty measure. It is greater if poverty is defined in relative terms, as half or 60 percent of the median family income, as in some European countries. America scores worse by this standard chiefly because we have more very high incomes, and thus a higher median income, than other advanced economies.[21]

The difference in welfare states is less than it appears. Among thirty higher-income countries, the United States spent only 16 percent of its gross domestic product on public social expenditures in 2005, compared to an average of 21 percent for all these countries. Sweden and France each spent 29 percent.[22] However, much of the "welfare state" in America is provided by private employers in the form of health care, pensions, and other benefits for their employees.[23] Also, the usual figures do not capture all in-kind benefits. With these adjustments, America spent 26 percent of gross domestic product on social benefits in 2001, which was not far below average among ten rich countries. America stands out not so much in spending less than other countries as in spending relatively more on in-kind benefits, especially health care, and less on cash aid.[24]

It is true that the United States lacks some benefits that are common in Europe. We do not usually create jobs for the long-term unemployed, and we do not guarantee everyone a minimum income in cash. The food stamps program is a virtually universal benefit for everyone below the poverty line, but we do not provide a cash income floor for individuals or families on an ongoing basis. Many European countries effectively do this by paying female-headed families more than we do and by allowing youth and the jobless to live on unemployment benefits indefinitely. American unemployment support is time limited, although currently, as stated earlier, it can last nearly two years.

In the short run, simply transferring more income to the poor does reduce measured poverty. That is largely what Europe has done. But in the longer term that policy fails. As long as the poor have no income of their own, government will strain to keep their incomes up with the growing wealth in the rest of society.[25] Unconditional aid also foments a lower class that is cut off from mainstream society, mainly by lack of employment. Fear of that was the main motive behind the dramatic American reform to enforce work in family welfare in the 1990s. The same fear is now driving Europe toward enforcing work in their programs for the employable. Academics would like America to accept entitlement as Europe traditionally did. In fact, the opposite is happening—America is teaching Europe to condition aid on work.[26]

Some think that the sharp division America makes

between social insurance and welfare causes us to shortchange the poor. Allegedly, programs for the poor tend to fail because they are poor programs. Intended only for the needy, they lack the wide support of programs such as Social Security that cover the broad population. Supposedly, the middle class will not pay higher taxes to improve programs from which it gets nothing. In this argument, it would be better to enact more universal programs that cover everyone, such as in health care, child care, or parental leave. Then the poor would gain along with everyone else without being singled out as different.[27] The recent enactment of a national health care system reflects thinking like this.

The trouble is that universal programs are vastly more costly than means-tested ones. The new national health system may prove unaffordable. And the political analysis here is mistaken. The middle class does not begrudge helping the poor. It does not expect to benefit from antipoverty programs directly. The criticism, rather, is that traditionally these programs were permissive. They did not promote working and self-reliance.[28] As we will see, that is changing.

America gains some advantages from giving the poor less direct aid. To afford what it does, Europe has to tax the private sector more than we do. It also regulates the labor market more heavily, making it more costly to hire workers and more difficult to dismiss them. America's less burdened economy generates more employment, especially for the low skilled. That is why immigrants stream here from around the world. America announces that the best way to overcome poverty here is to go to work in available jobs, stay there, and move up. Government will also help you if needed, but it will not replace individual effort. The private labor market is our most important social program. Even today, amid a slow recovery from recession, that remains true.

2

WHY ARE PEOPLE POOR?

A key question in helping the poor is why people become needy in the first place. The main debate is about the working-aged poor, and especially about why the parents of poor children seldom marry or work regularly. In Washington, nonwork is often blamed on impersonal economic forces. That is sometimes valid, particularly during bad economic times, as now. But it is much less true today than in the past.

This focus on the working-aged poor is recent. Traditionally, many of the poor were children or the elderly, whom society did not expect to provide for themselves. In 1959, 44 percent of the poor population was under age eighteen, and 14 percent was age sixty-five or over. The working aged, between those ages, were only 42 percent. Since then, however, the number of children in poverty has fallen as the nation has gotten richer and families have become smaller, reducing the number of children that parents must support. Elderly poverty has fallen due to increases in Social Security benefits. In 2009, only 35 percent of the poor were children, and only 8 percent were elderly. Well over half—57 percent—were working aged.[29]

NONMARRIAGE

What produces poverty among people in the prime of life? Two patterns overwhelmingly—nonmarriage and nonwork. Poor families typically arise when parents have children without marrying and then do not work regularly to support them. Usually, the father disappears

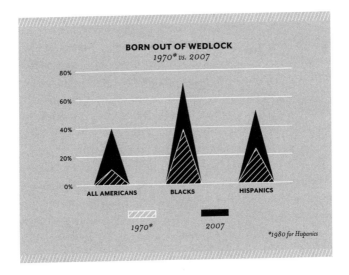

BORN OUT OF WEDLOCK
1970* vs. 2007

80%
60%
40%
20%
0%

ALL AMERICANS   BLACKS   HISPANICS

1970*   2007

*1980 for Hispanics

without paying child support, often due to failure to work. If the mother also fails to work, the family will end up on welfare, usually meaning TANF or SNAP.

Traditionally, American adults were expected to get through school, go to work, marry, and have children, in that order. This is what Haskins and Sawhill call the "success sequence." People who observe that ordering are very unlikely to be poor. If parents were seriously committed to each other before they had children, and if they worked more regularly to support the family, poverty would be far less prevalent than it is.[30] But today, more than ever in the past, poor adults have children first, work only irregularly, and seldom marry at all.

Of the two patterns, nonmarriage may appear more critical, as this is what initially creates a family at risk of poverty. But nonwork is at least as important. After children are born, whether the parents work determines whether the family in fact becomes poor. Employment compensates to some extent for parental nonmarriage or breakup. And it is only parents who work who are likely to marry and stay married in the first place.[31]

Nonmarriage has risen calamitously in recent decades. That is a major reason why poverty has persisted even as America has grown richer. Only 11 percent of American children were born out of wedlock in 1970, but by 2007 that rate had soared to 40 percent. For blacks, the comparable figures were 38 and 71 percent, respectively. For Hispanics, the figures were 24 percent in 1980, rising to 51 percent in 2007.[32] Higher unwed pregnancy is the principal reason why minorities suffer more poverty than whites. Nonmarriage also promotes inequality. Breakup has become common among poor and nonpoor alike. But among the college educated, marriage is still the norm, while among the less educated it is fading away. As Jonathan Rauch has written, "Marriage is displacing both income and race as the great class divide of the new century."[33]

NONWORK

Employment also is no longer the norm that it once was. In 1959, 68 percent of the heads of poor families worked at some level, and 31 percent worked full time and full

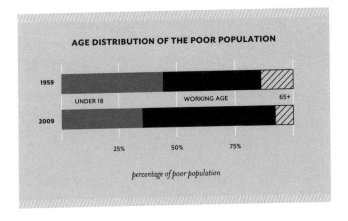

AGE DISTRIBUTION OF THE POOR POPULATION

1959

UNDER 18   WORKING AGE   65+

2009

25%   50%   75%

percentage of poor population

year. By 2009, those figures had plunged to 46 and 15 percent, respectively.[34] Much of the decline reflects growing real wages. As workers earned more, it became more difficult to work serious hours and remain under the poverty line, which does not rise as real incomes do. The poor became almost by definition people without regular employment.

However, there were also adverse social changes. The growth of welfare allowed many single mothers to live on aid without working. More low-income men retired early or went on disability programs where they did not have to work. Fewer men with only a high school education or less have been working or seeking work since at least 1979. For blacks that decline persisted even during good times in the 1990s.[35] In an earlier generation, people just like these would have been regular workers.

Meanwhile, employment rose in the rest of society. More mothers went to work alongside fathers in order to cover family budgets when the growth in incomes slowed in recent decades. The feminist movement caused women to take on more demanding careers. America became the most hard-working of Western nations.[36] As with marriage, a gulf opened between the lifestyle of the affluent and lower-income Americans.

Due to these trends, today's poor have largely separated from the labor force. Table 2 shows the share of persons aged sixteen and over who worked at various levels in 2009, first for the population as a whole and then for the poor. Figures are also shown for men, women, and several categories of family heads. The difference between the general society and the poor is stark. Nearly two-thirds of all adults worked at some level, 42 percent of them full time and full year, while below the poverty line the figures were only 36 and 9 percent, respectively. The story is much the same comparing average and poor men, women, or family heads. Among women heading families, around 70 percent were working in the population, more than 40 percent full time and full year, but among the poor barely half of female heads worked at all. If we compared the poor to the nonpoor, rather than to the general population, the gap would be larger still.

Table 3 shows poverty rates for the same work levels and demographic groups shown in table 2. The effect of work levels is dramatic. While the overall poverty rate for

TABLE 2. EMPLOYMENT STATUS OF PERSONS 16 AND OVER AND FAMILY HEADS, BY INCOME LEVEL, IN PERCENT, 2009

	PERSONS	MEN	WOMEN	ALL HEADS	FEMALE HEADS	ALL HEADS	FEMALE HEADS
						WITH CHILDREN UNDER 18	
All income levels							
Worked at any time	65	71	60	70	67	80	73
Full time / full year	42	48	35	49	42	56	45
Did not work	35	29	40	30	33	20	27
Income below poverty							
Worked at any time	36	41	32	46	48	53	52
Full time / full year	9	12	7	15	13	17	14
Did not work	64	59	68	54	52	47	48

Source: U.S. Bureau of the Census, March 2010 Annual Social and Economic Supplement, tables 14–15, 22.
Note: Full time means at least thirty-five hours a week, full year at least fifty weeks a year.

TABLE 3. POVERTY RATES BY EMPLOYMENT LEVEL OF PERSONS 16 AND OVER AND FAMILY HEADS, IN PERCENT, 2009

	PERSONS	MEN	WOMEN	ALL HEADS	FEMALE HEADS	ALL HEADS	FEMALE HEADS
						WITH CHILDREN UNDER 18	
Overall	12	11	14	11	30	17	38
Worked at any time	7	6	8	7	21	11	27
Full time / full year	3	3	3	3	9	5	12
Did not work	23	22	23	20	47	41	69

Source: U.S. Bureau of the Census, March 2010 Annual Social and Economic Supplement, tables 14–15, 22.

adults in 2009 was 12 percent, it was only 7 percent for those who worked at all, and only 3 percent for those working full time and full year—but 23 percent for those not working. Similar contrasts prevail across the table. For female heads with children, the general poverty rate was 38 percent, but it was only 12 percent for those fully employed—versus 69 percent for those not working at all. Many of these nonworkers would be on welfare. Admittedly, people who work more also are typically paid more, so they make more if they work. If one controlled for wage differences, the effect of work levels on poverty would be less dramatic. But it would still dominate. The lion's share of adult poverty is due, at least in the first instance, to low working levels.

POOR LIVES

Nonmarriage and nonwork, often continuing across generations, have chiefly formed the long-term poor population in America. The great fact about life in poor areas is that having children is far more certain than working. Poor youth often grow up in families that are female headed and nonworking, and then they themselves repeat that pattern. Children are not well prepared for school and so do poorly there, typically giving up on learning and dropping out before finishing high school. Among rich and poor alike, teenage girls and boys are drawn to sex. But among the better off, that urge is typically checked by strong families and involvement in school and college. Youth keep focused on getting ahead. The "success sequence" takes hold, with people postponing childbearing until after school, work, and marriage. Among the poor, however, parents typically exert much less control. Young people find their identity chiefly through peer groups outside both the home and school. Girls tend to get pregnant before marriage, often as teenagers, while boys join gangs, which are often involved in the drug trade. By these routes, women end up early as single mothers on welfare while men go to prison. Their wages are attached to pay support for children they have abandoned. Despite having children, neither men nor women usually attempt to marry or work regularly. That is the immediate reason they usually become poor.[37]

THE SEARCH FOR BARRIERS

How does one explain these adverse patterns? Typically, experts look for social barriers. The poor, they say, are blocked from working by impediments outside themselves, and this also discourages marriage. If the barriers were removed, work and marriage levels would rise. But research has failed to find barriers sufficient to support these claims.[38]

The Labor Market. The usual culprit is the labor market. One criticism focuses on low wages. It is easy to show that working full time at the minimum wage, now $7.25 an hour, will not enable one to support a family. But the minimum wage actually has little connection to

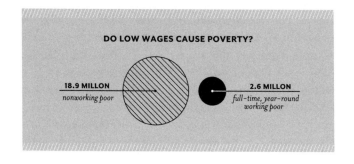

poverty. Most minimum-wage workers are not heads of household and are not poor. They live in families where other people are working. Nor do most poor adults, when they do work, earn only the minimum wage. They typically earn somewhat above that. They are poor mainly due to low working levels, not low wages.

Do low wages in general cause poverty? In 2009, 10.7 million people worked yet had incomes under the poverty line. Indeed, 2.6 million of them worked full time year round yet still were poor. These workers could use higher wages. Yet in most cases the working poor work less than normal hours, or they have large families where nobody else works. And they are considerably outnumbered by the nonworking poor—18.9 million in 2009.[39] Again, poverty is caused mostly by low working hours, not low wages.

Are workers discouraged from working by low wages? Would work levels rise if low-skilled workers could earn more? That sounds logical, yet research and experience do not support it. Government experiments in income maintenance from the 1960s through the 1980s showed that the work levels of heads of low-income households were largely unresponsive to wages. If anything, higher wages caused work levels to fall, as workers could now cover their family budgets with fewer working hours.[40] Poor adults typically do not come forward to join voluntary programs designed to help them work, even when subsidized jobs are offered, nor do these programs clearly raise work levels.[41] When low-skilled wages rose in the 1990s, poor mothers' work levels did rise, but this mainly reflected enforcing work due to welfare reform, as I discuss further below. Poor men were largely outside welfare, and their work levels improved little if at all.[42]

Are jobs simply unavailable to most poor adults? Many believe that the economy shed so many low-skilled jobs in recent decades due to deindustrialization that few remain. Actually, the economy continues to generate a great many unskilled jobs. According to the "mismatch theory," such jobs may exist, but they are typically located in the suburbs, not in the inner city where many poor families live. Of if there are city jobs, they demand more education than poor job seekers have.[43] But mismatch effects are not strong enough to explain the large work differences between the poor and the rest of society. By the 1990s, the success of welfare reform in employing poor mothers and runaway immigration from Latin America and Asia proved that unskilled jobs must still be plentiful, even in the cities.

Many would blame poverty simply on the current recession, which has raised the unemployment rate close to 10 percent. Poverty rose from 12.5 percent in 2007 to 14.3 percent in 2009, and much of that increase was no doubt due to the recession. Yet in good times and bad, *most* poor adults are not even in the labor force, so the recession little affects them. They are still struggling, but not notably because of the economy. The recession has hit the middle class far harder. They have often lost well-paying jobs that are hard to replace. But even in a recession, millions of low-skilled jobs are filled every month, and immigration continues.[44] State and local officials say that jobs are less available than in better times, but it is still reasonable to expect poor men and women to work.[45] Those made poor by hard times are only the icing on a large and nonworking cake.

It is true that, even if low-skilled jobs are available, they seldom pay enough for the holders to earn mainstream incomes. Across the economy, earnings and incomes have recently grown more unequal. Some think this has demoralized low-income people, causing many to give up on employment. But inequality and poverty are largely separate problems. Mostly, inequality has grown because high-income people are doing well, not because lower-income people are doing worse. Low-skilled jobs are still sufficient to avoid poverty and welfare for most families, provided both parents work. For the low-skilled, steady work in available jobs is still the best way forward. The private economy is still our most important safety net.

Single Mothers. Another approach has been to seek barriers in the lives of the poor single mothers at the center of the poverty problem. Even if jobs are available, perhaps poor mothers cannot take them because of having to care for children or their own limited skills.

The original rationale for welfare was that destitute mothers had to be given an income, for if they worked, their children would be neglected. Better-off mothers set that fear aside as they flooded to work in recent decades. Evaluations in the 1990s showed that putting welfare mothers in work programs actually has little effect on their children, either positive or negative.[46] Statistical studies suggest that the effect is positive, with low-income children doing better in school if their mothers work.[47] That effect may arise because working makes mothers more effective as parents or because being put in day care gives children more stimulation than staying home with a nonworking mother.

But perhaps mothers lack the child care they would need to work. Advocates suggest that only government care is adequate, but the system we have is mostly private and informal. In 2006, only 26 percent of poor children under age five with working mothers were in child care centers or other organized care; the others were cared for by relatives. Care is also cheaper on average than most people realize. In 2006, only 15 percent of poor working mothers with preschoolers paid anything at all for care; the others arranged care informally with friends and relatives. Those who paid for care spent an average of $73 a week.[48] To make sure poor mothers would be able to work, the government more than doubled child care funding between 1997 and 2006, from $5.3 to $12 billion (in constant 2006 dollars).[49] Yet research indicates that spending more on care has little effect on whether welfare mothers work.[50] That is apparently because the care they need is already available.[51]

The idea that welfare mothers were too unskilled to work was belied in the 1990s, when millions of them went to work after welfare reform was enacted. Jobs they could do were widely available, employers welcomed them, and they encountered only limited problems on the job.[52]

Thus, nonworking poverty cannot usually be blamed on external barriers. The poor themselves say as much. In 2009, only 12 percent of poor adults who did not work blamed this on their inability to find work. In 2007, before the recession, the figure was only 5 percent. In both years, this was the least common reason cited for not working. Much more often, respondents claimed illness, retirement, family responsibilities, or going to school as reasons.[53] For today's poor, the main impediments to working lie not in the society or economy but in private life.

Barriers are, in fact, far more important for workers than nonworkers. It is after people go to work that they truly confront limitations to opportunity. Those who work will inevitably have more trouble handling the logistics of employment, including child care, than those who do not. Those with education and skills will also earn much more than those without, and so on. No one pretends that low-skilled workers in America have an easy life. Liberals will see cause to intervene in the society, while conservatives will argue that an unrestrained economy offers the best hope to improve jobs, incomes, and advancement for all. I do not take sides in that debate. My point, rather, is that the problems that workers and nonworkers have are very different. The challenges workers encounter on the job usually cannot explain why so few poor adults work at all.

The Marriage Mystery. As for the breakdown of marriage, specific external causes are even more difficult to identify. Why should it be harder for adults to form long-term marital bonds today than it was decades ago? Recessions like the recent one do put strain on marriages, but this cannot explain the long-term trend against marriage. Researchers tend to blame the problem on impersonal economic changes. Low wages or lack of jobs, they reason, lowers income and stresses families, or it makes men less marriageable. So does rising incarceration among low-income men, especially blacks. But the evidence for all these theories is weak.[54]

Supposedly, in the globalizing economy low-skilled workers make less secure incomes than they once did. They say they cannot make enough to meet the standards they set for marriage, so they prefer to cohabitate rather than marrying formally.[55] It is hard to credit this reasoning, however, because incomes are still much higher today than they were decades or a century ago when marriage was stronger and cohabitation was rare. And even if conditions were worse, cohabitation is not a sensible response. As long as couples still have children, as is likely, they still incur the major burdens of marriage. Even if fathers decline to marry or disappear, they must still pay child support. And parents who cohabitate break up more often than if they were married, exposing both themselves and their children to lower income and poverty. Faced with insecurity, men and women would do better to avoid all procreation. Or they should marry and stick together through thick and thin, as most adults used to do.

The decline of marriage is more plausibly due to change not in the economy but in culture. For obscure reasons, many people no longer feel that marriage is a condition of carrying on intimate relationships, and unwed pregnancy no longer bears the stigma it once did. The decay of marriage, like other social norms, may reflect a society with rising incomes, where social discipline no longer seems so necessary as in the past. The decline of marriage, after all, began in the 1960s, when the society enjoyed the greatest wealth it had ever known.[56]

Culture and Authority. Researchers continue to search for barriers, but most have been driven over time toward a cultural understanding of poverty. Sociologists in the 1960s spoke of a culture of poverty, a defeated mindset where poor adults believe in work, marriage, and other mainstream values, but they commonly have given up living by them. The reason is usually not limitations of opportunity but the inability of the poor to commit themselves to their own goals for a successful life. Too often they are deflected away from work, marriage, or law-abidingness by the confusions of private life or the temptations of the "street" and the drug culture.

Poor women esteem marriage highly, but despite this they tend to have children young with men they are involved with yet refuse to marry. The reason is usually not that they lack birth control or any external resource. Rather, it is that they do not trust their men to support them, to play the role of husband and father. So, feeling that marriage is beyond them, they settle for single motherhood.[57] For their part, the men also hope for a conventional married life, but they typically fail to do the things this requires, such as getting through school and securing a steady job. Many are distracted from domesticity by an alluring street culture that promises a fast life and high incomes from the drug trade. So they never become the steady workers their partners want. Just as with the mothers, their actual life violates their own values.[58]

To believe in a culture of poverty does not mean to hold the poor personally responsible for their problems, that is, "to blame the victims."[59] Quite the contrary, for the essence of that culture is precisely that it lacks a sense of individual responsibility. People feel overwhelmed by problems over which they feel they have no control. A defeatist culture is as much a structural impediment to work or marriage as any feature of the economy or the larger society. For that very reason, government must take the lead in combating it—by both assisting the poor to work and expecting them to do so.

The barriers approach assumes that the poor are unfree, faced with unusual constraints. The cultural approach suggests rather that they are *too* free. Although the poor feel defeated, society has allowed them ways to avoid functioning that other people lack. It has failed to uphold its own norms. It no longer tells the poor clearly what they are expected to do. Traditional welfare and social programs, with their society-blaming rhetoric, allow them to project all problems on the environment. Good behavior that would serve their interests, including marrying and working, is left too much to choice. The better off usually avoid the same problems because they are *less* free. They might have more resources and better opportunities, but they are also surrounded by authority figures—parents, teachers, and employers, for example— who tell them constantly what to do. Compared to the poor, they have not so much more rights as more obligations.[60]

American poverty in recent decades might chiefly be traced to the culture of poverty and permissive public policies. It is not an economic problem so much as a problem of public authority. In the 1960s and 1970s, American government, acting for the society, no longer enforced civilities such as working and obeying the law with the stringency it once did. So crime, welfare, nonwork, and other social disorders mushroomed. In a rich society, poverty means not deprivation of resources but a breakdown of order. The solution must be to restore order.

TRENDS IN POLICY

The development of antipoverty policy since the 1960s confirms this interpretation. Over time, society learned— or relearned—that it could not overcome poverty just by subsidizing the poor. It also had to expect better behavior from them. The solution was not help alone, nor the denial of help, but a combination of help and hassle.

Poverty first became a national issue in the 1960s, in the shadow of the civil rights movement. One of the triggers was the publication of Michael Harrington's *The Other America*, which publicized a deprived face of society that had been hidden.[61] Policymakers initially blamed poverty largely on racial discrimination. Solutions stressed expansions of opportunity, and indeed the civil rights reforms did much to reduce poverty by helping low-paid blacks get better jobs. The emphasis was on building up benefits for groups perceived as deprived, which included racial minorities and women as well as the poor. States raised family welfare benefits (which they control), and new benefits such as Medicaid and food stamps were enacted. The behavioral side of poverty was ignored.

By the early 1970s, most of the working poor had escaped poverty. That left a largely nonworking poor behind, with which we still struggle. In the 1960s and 1970s, the work problem was blamed largely on low skills. It was assumed that if poor youth and adults could improve their education and credentials, they would earn more and also work more. But, as mentioned earlier, conventional education and training programs accomplished little. Clients who went through them did not work or earn much more afterward than they did before.

Some economists pointed to adverse incentives. Given low wages, the poor seemed to have little reason to work. Welfare benefits also deterred work because they were means tested. Anything the recipients did earn was deducted from their grants, leaving them no better off. To counter this, starting in 1967 welfare added work incentives: recipients who worked were allowed to keep part of their earnings free of any grant reduction. That made working more remunerative. In 1975, the EITC was enacted, adding a direct subsidy to low-wage work. But welfare work incentives had no effect on work levels, and the EITC had no large effect until the 1990s. The main reason is probably that the seriously poor are less calculating than economists suppose. If they were economically rational, they would never have engaged in the patterns that made most of them poor—unwed pregnancy and nonwork. They would never have been poor for very long in the first place.

In the 1970s, the economy was troubled, and some argued that jobs were unavailable to the poor. There was a brief vogue for creating jobs in government, and Washington funded as many as 750,000 positions. But these programs also evaluated poorly, failing to transition most of their clients into work in the private sector. They ended in 1981. Again, the programs were voluntary, with no power to command work. Government still construed work as a benefit for the needy and not as an obligation.

The attempt to solve the work problem by economic means was a failure. No new benefit, service, or incentive was discovered that, once provided, caused nonworkers to rush thankfully into jobs. In the 1980s, many conservatives argued that social programs were doing more harm than good and should simply be cut. Under the Reagan administration, some cuts were made, but social problems continued to grow. Simply spending less on the poor, like spending more, did not reach to the heart of the poverty problem.[62] These disappointments led toward welfare reform and other directive programs, which I discuss further below. Those programs have attempted to link practical help for the poor with efforts to redirect lifestyle. That combination has been more successful than anything that came before.

3

CRITICAL PERSPECTIVES

How should we respond to the poverty problem and to what government has done about it? No issue is more controversial in Washington. Although the poor are relatively few in number, how best to help them is the subject of heated debate among the better off. That is partly because our religious traditions make helping the poor a priority. I explore these below. Believers are supposed to reach out to the poor, and society should also make some collective provision for them.

At the same time, what that requires in practice is not settled by the sacred texts. It depends on the circumstances of each time and place. Close study is needed to determine what actually helps the poor in practice. The nub of dispute is especially how to deal with the behavioral side of poverty. How should government and religious believers respond to the fact that, at least in the first instance, so many poor contribute to their own predicament?

Here I summarize perspectives from secular ideologies and our religious traditions. I include my own reading of the Gospels as they relate to poverty as well as two influential traditions—Catholic social teaching and the new social gospel—that are much more critical of existing policy.

POLITICAL IDEOLOGIES

The most obvious approaches to poverty derive from the secular ideologies that structure American politics. Traditionally, liberals have wanted government to do more about a range of domestic problems, not only poverty, while conservatives want it to do less. Many debates about poverty and welfare in Congress and state legislatures fall into this pattern. The poverty question, however, has tended to evoke particularly extreme versions of both of these perspectives.

The Rights Tradition. At one extreme, advocates for the poor assert that our obligation is simply to do more for the poor with no questions asked. The poor should qualify for aid on the basis of impersonal economic criteria, and how they live should be ignored. That is the position called entitlement. In this view, the needy have a right to more income and services simply because they are worse off than the average. In American politics, when a group seems to lack benefits or opportunities that other people have, demands are made for redress. The claimants deny any responsibility for their predicament.

Movements with claims like this helped create the American welfare state. Social programs to aid the vulnerable began to develop during the Progressive era over a century ago, mostly at the state and local levels, as the nation grappled with the growth of large cities, industry, and immigration. During the Great Depression of the 1930s, the first large national benefit programs arose in response to mass unemployment. And during the 1960s and 1970s, many new antipoverty programs were enacted largely in response to the claims of black Americans for more equal opportunity. Some of those programs did indeed reduce poverty and insecurity.

The builders of the welfare state developed the idea that access to social benefits should be seen as an aspect of citizenship. Just as Americans are entitled to fair legal treatment and political rights, so they should be guaranteed aid and other social benefits when they are jobless, ill, or retired. A democratic society should guarantee people a widening freedom where they are protected against many vicissitudes of private life.[63]

The rights tradition persuades, however, only if the difficulties people face really are external to them, such as economic breakdown or Jim Crow laws. After the 1960s, such conditions became rare. The nation became much richer, so destitution became unusual. And because of past reforms favoring workers and nonwhites, few people who worked regularly remained poor for long. Yet in this new world, social problems among the poor grew more serious rather than less so. Unwed pregnancy, dependency on welfare, school failure, and substance abuse all escalated. Crime rose while work levels fell. This was the genesis of today's poverty problem. It led eventually to the efforts to enforce work and other civilities that I describe below.

Libertarianism. At the other extreme are libertarians who say that government should do nothing special for the poor. The needy should be assured only the same protections and opportunities as other citizens. Some libertarians think that aid to the poor must be voluntary because government has no right to tax other people to help them.[64] Others believe that public antipoverty programs are counterproductive, either because their cost depresses economic growth and thus jobs, harming opportunities for the poor to support themselves, or because such programs tend inherently to reward bad behavior. If welfare supports female-headed families who do not work, on this logic, it will inevitably create more such families. So aid to the poor is best left to private charity.[65]

From a religious viewpoint, however, moral commandments come ahead of property rights. While the biblical tradition respects private property, it does in principle permit some transfer of wealth from the better off to help the less fortunate. That is implicit in the prophets' call to the authorities to do more to succor the needy. While the responsibility to help the poor rests on private individuals and organizations, in our tradition government also accepts a duty to aid the needy. So the libertarian stance is one that many believers will question.

Research also has not shown that social problems like nonemployment or unwed pregnancy result chiefly from the economic incentives set up by welfare. It is indeed true that liberal social programs have been counterproductive, but that is chiefly because they are permissive, giving no clear guidance about how recipients ought to behave. The disincentives they create against good behavior are part of this larger problem.

RELIGIOUS TRADITIONS

More helpful than these secular positions are our
religious traditions.[66] These are far less abstract than
political ideologies. They focus not on generalities about
who should get aid but on how best to help people in
a concrete society. The emphasis is on aiding the needy
in practical ways, but also on the reaffirmation of
community. That implies that the poor get assistance,
but also that they must fulfill community norms such as
work.

Ancient Israel. In Old Testament times, Israel combined
generosity toward the poor with clear demands for
functioning.[67] Able-bodied families or individuals who
fell on hard times were allowed to borrow money from
the community on generous terms, but the loans were
expected to be repaid, and outright grants were avoided.
The dependent poor, who could not support themselves,
such as widows and orphans, received some food without
charge, but they had to work for it by gleaning in the
fields. So far as possible, the needy worked for aid in
order to minimize stigma, and elders could even create
jobs to be sure there was enough work for all. Every seven
years, debts that had not been repaid were remitted, and
every forty-nine years, families that had lost their land
recovered it.

Old Testament scriptures clearly call the authorities
to be compassionate. They are to be generous, even as
God was generous to the Jewish people by liberating them

from Egypt. Everything humans have in life is ultimately a gift from God. At the same time, those who received aid faced clear accountability. Dependency did not free them from normal social pressures to function. To be sure, we are uncertain how fully these norms were treated as obligatory and how far they were realized in practice. But the emphasis on community and reciprocity is clear.

In the Jewish tradition, there was no compunction about using public authority and funding to provide what we would call welfare. At the same time, the ancient system remained largely informal. It depended on the ability of families to take care of their own, and on a private economy to generate wealth. Those institutions also generated pressures to function. Welfare never replaced the family or private employment, but built upon them.

The Prophets. In the later Old Testament, the prophets appear as enforcers of this Hebrew tradition. They upbraid religious and political authorities for neglect of the needy. These denunciations are often scathing. God, in Amos's words, declares that "I despise your feasts, and I take no delight in your solemn assemblies." He rejects Israel's "burnt offerings." "But let justice roll down like waters, and righteousness like an ever-flowing stream."[68] The judgments, however, are one-sided. We never hear the response from the establishment. The prophets suggest that helping the poor mainly requires good intentions. The authorities would no doubt say more about the difficulty of helping the poor, and solutions would not seem so simple.

And when we read the prophets today, we lose much of the sense of social context given by the earlier Hebrew texts (chiefly from the Pentateuch) that set out society's obligations. The judgments rain down from on high, but we forget the strong sense of mutual obligation that Israel derived from its religious laws. Expectations to do good rested on everyone, rich and poor alike, and not only on the privileged, whom the prophets criticize. That made it possible for society to assuage the needy without fear that, in doing so, its cohesion would be threatened. Our situation today is very different.

NEW TESTAMENT

The New Testament repeats the social teaching of the Old. Like the prophets, Jesus praises assistance to the poor, and he indicts religious leaders for indifference. They are the "blind guides" who prize religious ceremony but neglect "the weightier matters of the law, justice and mercy and faith."[69] Jesus's message, like the prophets', often seems unilateral, as if he laid obligations only on the rich and powerful.

But fortunately, the Gospel stories restore much of the context that we lose in the prophets. We get to go behind Jesus's words to the relationships he had with his followers. We find that he is true to Israel's ancient tradition of community. In his world, aid to the poor is not unilateral, nor is it only economic. Three ideals can be discerned in his words and deeds.

Sustenance. First, Jesus aids people in immediate, practical terms. He spends much of his ministry helping people in trouble. He never suggests that they do not need or deserve help in some form. Yet he does not concentrate on material need. Indeed, he says very little about poverty in this modern sense. He never suggests that low income per se is an emergency or that the rich owe the poor some general recompense. He calls for no social programs, no redistribution. Indeed, he criticizes conventional alms-giving.[70]

Nor is helping the poor one-sided, as it tends to be today. Jesus expects those he helps to participate in overcoming their problems. He does not counsel self-help. On the other hand, he does not save nameless poor people whom other people tell him are in trouble, as today's advocates expect government to do. Rather, the distressed generally have to approach him personally and *ask* for help.[71] He also asks petitioners directly what they want, and he expects an answer. He is offended if they make no response or if they try to get his help without facing him.[72] Furthermore, he also expects those he helps to show *"faith."* By this he means not only to believe in him but to affirm the meaningfulness of life in some larger sense.[73] To him, the poor are never passive victims who have no responsibility for themselves.

Reciprocity. A second goal is reciprocity. Today's approach to poverty focuses narrowly on economic deprivation. In the Bible, however, the poor are not simply needy but *outcasts*—outside respectable society. This is chiefly because they are seen to have violated social or religious mores. This reflected the same concerns about "deservingness" that still surround poverty today. Thus, to overcome poverty, it is not enough to assuage material need. One must also restore the poor to community. That means facing the deservingness questions rather than avoiding them. It requires effort by *both* the society and the poor themselves.

Many commentators interpret Jesus as a partisan figure, who takes the side of the poor against the better off. That is the view of Latin American liberation theologians, for example.[74] Certainly, he befriends the marginalized as few in his society dared to do. Nothing communicates the Good News so powerfully as this. If even the poor are acceptable to the Son of Man, a new age has indeed begun. Yet it is too strong to say that Jesus identifies with the poor *against* the rest of society. In background, he himself was neither poor nor privileged.[75] He heals all manner of people with apparent indifference to whether they are rich or poor. He has a ministry to the rich as well as the poor. He spends much of his time interacting with Pharisees, Sadducees, and other members of the elite. He challenges their prejudices, but he wants to save them as well as the poor. In Old Testament language, he is neither "partial to the poor" nor does he "defer to the great."[76]

The poor in Jesus's time were far more likely than in ours to be victims of circumstance. Most often, those Jesus helps suffer from dread diseases. But despite this, he does not treat them as innocent victims. As noted above, he expects them to *ask* for his help and to show *faith*. And after he has healed them, he usually *admonishes* them. He directs them to discharge the religious rituals connected with healing, or he tells them not to publicize what he has done for them.[77] In two cases he tells them not to sin again, and in another instance he remarks that healing and forgiveness are the same.[78] His followers—like everyone—are sinners who need some direction in order to live well.

The best indication we have in the Gospels of how Jesus would respond to today's seriously poor occurs at the Pool of Bethesda in Jerusalem. The legend was that an angel periodically troubled the waters, and then whoever got into the pool first was healed of any infirmities. Jesus encounters a man who has been lying by the pool for thirty-eight years. He must have lived by begging. Jesus first confronts him with his demand to *ask*: "Do you want to be healed?" But the man does not answer. Rather, he complains that no one will help him into the pool when the angel comes. He cannot imagine why what *he* wants should matter. It is the defeatism, the denial of agency, typical of the seriously poor. But Jesus abruptly commands, "Rise, take up your pallet, and walk." Startled, the man gets up. He is *healed*. Later, Jesus

confronts him again with the *admonition*, "See, you are
well! Sin no more, that nothing worse befall you."[79]

This was not the unjudging solicitude that many
see in Jesus. Yet he did do for this man what he most
required. When people refuse to take responsibility for
themselves, the command to function is what they most
need to hear. The key to Jesus's ministry is not *redistribution*
but *relationship*. The duty of those who follow him is not
simply to bail out the poor but to *relate* to them on an
ongoing basis—to welcome them into mainstream society
but also to expect from them the normal civilities of that
society. By relating to both rich and poor and calling
both to their duties, Jesus knits up society's divisions and
offers his followers a glimpse of the Kingdom of God.

Autonomy. A third goal is autonomy. Jesus seeks that the
poor, like other people, should be self-reliant. He does
not mean that they should necessarily make no demands
on government, as libertarians want. Nor does he seek, as
in the rights tradition, to liberate them from constraint.
In the biblical tradition, freedom is never license.
Rather, to be free is to obey God's will and nothing but.
It is to resist unjust authority but also to avoid sin, which
means enslavement to impulse. In the Episcopalian
phrase, God's "service is perfect freedom."[80] As Jesus
states during his temptation, "Man shall not live by bread
alone, but by every word that proceeds from the mouth
of God." The Christian ideal, Paul wrote, is to become
"mature" in this same way, to achieve "the stature of the

fullness of Christ."[81]

In modern thinking, the welfare state should emancipate people from the constraints of private life, including the pressure to work. But in the biblical vision, standards for good behavior—what the Bible calls the "law"—are maintained. The poor find these strictures hard to fulfill. Jesus is sometimes said to have attacked or repealed the law in order to liberate the poor. He does strongly advocate mercy and forgiveness. He counsels his followers to judge not that they be not judged. Those whom God forgives should likewise forgive others, even seventy times seven.[82]

Yet he does not question the law itself. He says he comes to fulfill it, not to abolish it.[83] The laws that he challenges are cultic rules governing what Jews could eat and forbidding healing on the Sabbath. Jesus never questions the more important laws governing social behavior, which have much more to do with stigmatizing the poor. He specifically embraces the Golden Rule and the Ten Commandments, with their prohibitions against theft, murder, and adultery.[84] In the Bible, the poor are forgiven for violating social standards, but not exempted from them. To forgive people without also expecting good behavior is what Dietrich Bonhoeffer called "cheap grace."[85]

Scriptures also specifically affirm the obligation to work that is at the core of the poverty debate. From the fall in the Garden of Eden, God commanded that humans work. Jesus says that he works alongside the Father.[86] Paul cites his own labors as an example to others. Some of his followers imagined that they need not work because Jesus's second coming was imminent. Paul retorts that they must "earn their own living, for "if any one will not work, let him not eat."[87]

Aid and Expectations. In the New Testament, like the Old, helping the poor is a priority, but helping means primarily to restore the poor to community rather than simply to subsidize or liberate them. The community is based on mutual expectations about good behavior. Poverty represents a breakdown where, typically, the society has neglected the needy, but the latter have also infringed social norms in ways that alienate others. The commandment is to rebuild community through doing more to help but also by expecting better behavior from those aided. Assistance is not a substitute for engagement. The answer to poverty is not redistribution but the rebuilding of relationships with the poor where both sides give and receive.

As against the political ideologies, we should not give aid to the poor as a matter of right, but neither should we deny it to them in principle. Properly understood, the biblical commandment is not to spend more or less on the poor. Rather, it is to do what they most require. That will likely mean aiding them in practical ways, as it has throughout history. But it will also mean confronting the lifestyles that help to make people poor. Helping the seriously poor requires challenging them, as well as compassion. Levying expectations is a crucial form of caring. Americans of the Victorian era understood this truth better than we do. It is even more important in today's relatively affluent and secure society.[88]

This position is close to the views of most Americans. Ordinary people sense in their bones both that helping the poor is a priority *and also* that the poor must help themselves. Some will ask, how can we do both? If we help the poor, they are not self-reliant, and if they are self-reliant we do not help them. But the two priorities conflict only in political ideology. In local anti-poverty efforts, it is quite possible to combine them. Programs help the poor the most, in fact, when they move them toward greater independence, as I show further below.

RESPONSES TO JESUS

The potential of a biblical vision, however, has not been reaped, because the leading religious forces in the poverty debate have strayed from that heritage. Much as in the rights tradition, they characterize the poor mostly as helpless victims of whom nothing can be expected. On this basis, there never can be community and thus a true solution to the poverty problem.

Catholic Social Teaching. The Catholic Church strongly influenced discussions of poverty and welfare reform in the 1980s and 1990s. Since 1891, the popes have issued several encyclicals on the problems of poverty and inequality in Western societies.[89] American Catholic bishops issued the pastoral letter *Economic Justice for All* in 1986, and it applies a similar perspective to poverty in America.[90]

These statements reflect a social democratic vision, born in Europe in the nineteenth century, that identifies the poor with the working class and views capitalism as a threat to it. Like Marx and his socialist heirs, Catholic theologians still stress the insecurities of the industrial economy, the fact that it might fail to support all willing workers and their families. Thus, government must intervene to civilize wages and working conditions. Yet since the nineteenth century, capitalism had done more to eradicate destitution, in this country and abroad, than any other institution.

In their statements, Catholic leaders are also credulous in believing that the poor are still hedged around with other barriers, such as racism, that prevent them from supporting themselves. The documents fail to take seriously the evidence, cited above, showing that outside impediments generally cannot explain nonwork among the poor on the scale we see. Catholics and other advocates continue to call for more child care and other benefits when there is little evidence that they would raise work levels, although they would make people better off. The Catholic tradition treats the poor as workers blocked from employment by the society. In fact, most are nonworkers, and merely enlarging the opportunity to work will not change that.

In the encyclicals and in *Economic Justice for All*, there is no serious discussion of the behavioral side of poverty. To speak of nonmarriage or nonwork is discouraged as reflecting "misunderstandings and stereotypes."[91] The bishops, like the popes, affirm that work for the employable poor is expected, but society must create conditions to make sure work is possible. Thus, employment is treated mostly as a benefit that society must ensure to the poor, and all the specific obligations are shifted to the nonpoor or to government. Especially, government must not expect single mothers to work outside the home—the very demand that welfare reform was to make in the 1990s.

Catholics avoid rigid claims to rights, and yet their vision is founded on a profound moral inequality. In the world we have, the bishops say, the rich stand above the poor. But rather than summon both sides to a new community, they declare a preferential "option for the poor." "A constant biblical refrain is that the poor must be cared for and protected and that when they are exploited, God hears their cries." Thus, "a community is measured by its treatment of the powerless."[92] Hierarchy is not devalued before God but retained and inverted. The poor become the judges of the society. All of the onus for change is shifted to the better off. They can now justify themselves only if they serve the disadvantaged. No serious attention is paid to the common obligations, such as working or obeying the law, that define a community.

The New Social Gospel. Protestant groups have been even more one-sided. Their stance toward poverty goes back to the "social gospel" movement of the early twentieth century. Protestant reformers, outraged by the slums of American cities, demanded that society immediately devote much more attention to the poor than it had during the Gilded Age. In practice, these churchmen operated as the religious wing of the Progressive movement, supporting its early efforts to regulate industrialism and clean up local government.

Their central idea was that society had never taken seriously the social vision of the Gospels, but it should now do so. In Jesus's conception and in its early years, the church had been an egalitarian community that held property in common and radically devalued social and class differences. But too readily it had become an institution that accepted the world as it was, or—in the monastic orders—escaped from it. For the laity, religion became a matter of private piety, removed from politics. But now a direct connection should be restored between faith and politics, and earnest Christians should remake the world.[93]

The movement faded after the Progressive Era but was revived during the civil rights movement of the 1950s and 1960s. Many Protestant clergy, as well as Catholics and Jews, marched behind Dr. Martin Luther King, Jr. In liberal evangelicals such as Jim Wallis, the idea reappears that the Gospel supplies a relatively simple template for a just society. Its demands for attention to the poor and its strictures against pride and excessive wealth should simply be applied to the unequal and plutocratic society we have. There are endless good causes for greater equality at home and abroad in which believers should enlist. Especially, racism is an original sin for which white society must show continuing repentance. King and Nelson Mandela in South Africa are exemplars of justice for our time.[94]

Moral inequality is even stronger than in Catholic social teaching. The evangelical left seizes repeatedly on the image of the last judgment that appears in Matthew 25. There Jesus imagines himself sitting on a throne at the end of time, deciding who will go to heaven and who to hell. All that counts is whether people succored the unfortunate or not.[95] That seems to assign to the better off an awesome burden that they—and only they—must discharge if they are to be saved. "Nobody gets to heaven without a letter of reference from the poor," says James Forbes, pastor of Riverside Church, an affluent liberal congregation in New York.[96] As Ron Sider puts it, if the affluent "do not feed the hungry and clothe the naked, they go to hell."[97] Accordingly, to Nicholas Wolterstorff the poor have "rights" to income, health care, and so on that they may assert against the society, without apology—a formulation that mimics the secular rights tradition.[98]

But in these abstract pronouncements, the biblical sense of concrete community and reciprocity is lost. Wallis admits that poverty has behavioral causes, Wolterstorff that support rights might be forfeited if one does not work, but these are only asides.[99] As in Catholic doctrine, all the specific burdens for change are levied on the better off. They are called upon to fund much more aid and other benefits for the poor, as if this would itself solve the problems of the ghetto, which have far more to do with behavior. The difficult problems of fitting the poor back into community are ignored. The social gospel tradition appears more interested in judging the society than in actually helping the poor.

The Problem of Responsibility. The problem with both the Catholic tradition and the new social gospel is that the poor disappear as concrete human beings. They tend to be defined entirely by their disadvantages so that in practice they are not responsible for anything. That is contrary to the vision we see in both the Old and New Testaments.

The biblical tradition is indeed solicitous toward the poor, but it is not protective. There are still expectations about good behavior that apply to everyone, including the needy. In rights-oriented thinking, the poor are not so much forgiven as exempted from those rules. It is thought improper even to expect them to fulfill normal obligations, such as obeying the law or supporting one's family, because of the adversities they face. In the biblical tradition, rather, the poor are to be forgiven generously and repeatedly, but conventional norms still apply. They are offered not exemption but forgiveness based on redirecting their lives.

In the biblical tradition, the purpose is not to assign fault or blame. Rather, the focus is on change, on the future, not the past. Repentance means not to grovel in shortcomings, but to turn one's life around. Faults are recognized only so that they may be abandoned and a new life begun. To admit them is already to have stepped beyond them, to recognize the person God intends one to be.

4

WELFARE REFORM

The trends in policy that I surveyed earlier culminated in welfare reform. As explained above, "welfare" largely means the program of cash aid to needy children and single mothers originally called Aid to Families with Dependent Children. This program drew more scrutiny than any other because welfare mothers—and their absent partners—seemed particularly undeserving. Above all, few adult welfare recipients worked. In the background was the low employment found among poor adults in general, both on and off welfare.

Reform largely meant efforts to raise work levels among recipients. That struggle posed a test for competing theories about the causes of poverty and also for the critical perspectives I have summarized. After voluntary methods failed, government took to enforcing work. Welfare was transformed, and there was a trend toward greater order in society generally. This progress showed that poverty was, as I have suggested, due more to weak public expectations than to deficiencies of opportunity.

Secular ideologies and religious critics alike failed to anticipate the new welfare system that emerged, combining greater help with clearer work expectations. Far more prescient was the biblical tradition as I have described it.

STEPS TOWARD REFORM

In the 1960s and 1970s, work on welfare was promoted mainly by voluntary means. One of these was work incentives—allowing working recipients to keep part of their earnings to offset the disincentive to work, as explained earlier. The government also expanded training programs so that unskilled workers could get better jobs. In the 1970s, it even created jobs on a large scale. But none of these efforts had much effect. None caused more welfare mothers to go to work in the private economy, which is what they had to do to escape welfare and poverty.

Administrative Work Tests. The way forward lay in a different direction—administrative work tests. Since 1967, welfare mothers who were judged employable were in theory required to participate in work programs as a condition of aid. If they failed to do so, their benefits would be reduced or canceled. Work tests were at first more symbolic than real. The rules required mothers to participate only when their youngest child reached six years of age, later three years of age, and this exempted half or more of the caseload. Even after participation became mandatory (that is, a condition of aid), initially all the mothers had to do was register with the work program. If they were assigned to any activity, it was usually education or training, not actual work. And administration was loose, allowing many recipients to slip through the cracks and continue on aid without participation. So until the late 1980s, the percent of mothers working while on AFDC never exceeded 16 percent.[100]

State Experiments. By the 1980s, pressure to expect work increased. Federal rules were changed to allow states to experiment with more demanding work programs. Several states, led by California and Wisconsin, began to obligate a higher share of welfare mothers to enter work programs. Some also shifted the activity required away from education and training and toward actual work. Mothers, that is, were required to take available jobs, even if low wage, rather than studying in hopes of getting better positions later, a policy called work first. Local officials learned how to provide child care and other support services more quickly and efficiently so that more mothers could be made active.

Furthermore, some of these new work programs were positively evaluated. They increased the share of mothers going to work and also raised their earnings. Programs in San Diego were particularly influential.[101] The evaluations, done mostly by the Manpower Demonstration Research Corporation (MDRC), convinced policymakers because they were especially rigorous. Most earlier evaluations had not really established what social programs achieved. MDRC used an experimental methodology, where clients were randomly assigned either to the tested program or to a control group. This made the two groups truly equivalent and meant that any difference in outcomes between them could be reliably attributed to the program.

Work Enforcement. On average, the gains in employment and earnings from welfare work programs were larger than seen in most earlier education and training programs. That was mostly because the new programs were mandatory. They had a power to compel work by making it a condition of aid, which the earlier programs lacked. That caused more of the most disadvantaged mothers to come forward and participate, and they gained the most from doing so. Furthermore, results improved as the new programs became more demanding over the 1980s. The higher the share of welfare mothers who were obligated to participate, the higher the share who went to work.

At first it was unclear whether programs focused on education and training or on actual work were more effective. In the 1990s, a California evaluation and a large national study settled that work first was best. Even over five years, programs that put mothers to work in available jobs generated more gains in employment and earnings than those that tried to improve their skills. Training could still play a role, but it had to be short term and aimed at specific jobs. The widespread practice of allowing mothers to go to college on welfare was counterproductive.[102]

My own studies of welfare work programs showed that putting welfare mothers to work was principally an administrative challenge. It depended mainly on obligating the mothers to engage in regular activity outside the home. Once required to do this and provided with child care, they usually could and would work. The availability of jobs and the skills of the clients also mattered, but less so.[103] Along with the evaluations, these results confirmed that poverty was due mostly to a lack of public authority, not adverse economic or social conditions.

Reform came to center on work enforcement because this was the only approach to employment that worked. Another reason was politics. In welfare, the public demand that poor adults work was particularly intense. People felt not necessarily that recipients should leave aid—but that they should work alongside the taxpayers on whom they relied.

Personal Responsibility and Work Opportunity Reconciliation Act. The development of welfare work generated no major change in welfare until the 1990s. That was chiefly because Democrats controlled Congress. Since the 1960s, they had rebuffed repeated demands to cut or work-test welfare, calling them racist or hostile to the poor. However, in the early 1990s, there was a further increase in the welfare rolls, which reached over fourteen million people, due chiefly to rising unwed pregnancy. Public opinion turned even more strongly against AFDC.

Elected leaders responded. Bill Clinton won the presidency in 1992, in part by promising to "end welfare as we know it." Then in 1994, the Republicans won control of Congress for the first time in forty years. Welfare reform was a key plank of the Contract with America, the election platform of House Republicans.

Armed with a public mandate, in 1996 Congress enacted the Personal Responsibility and Work Opportunity Reconciliation Act (PRWORA) and forced Bill Clinton to sign it. PRWORA was the most radical reform in the history of welfare. Above all, it ended entitlement. Aid was no longer to be given to people simply on the basis of need. It was now to be conditioned seriously on work.

AFDC was recast as TANF. The new program required states to put half their cases in work activities by 2002—a much higher level than before—or face cuts in their federal funding. They could count any decline in their caseloads against that target, because cases leaving welfare would typically go to work. PRWORA also redefined the permissible work activities to stress work first rather than education and training. And it limited welfare families to five years on the rolls, timed from the signing of the act in 1996. It was the combination of long-standing public feeling with the turning of the political tide in Washington that finally unleashed this radical reform.[104]

The Implementation of Reform. Compared to earlier antipoverty programs, TANF was implemented unusually rapidly and well. PRWORA gave states wide leeway about details—one of its points was to reverse the centralization of welfare policy in Washington. But most states shared the new act's focus on employment and work first, and they received ample funding from Washington.

Some states implemented the act better than others.

The exemplars were mostly northern states such as Wisconsin, which had deep good-government traditions. Urban states such as New York and Pennsylvania were more politically divided about reform, while some in the South suffered from weak administration.[105] Yet virtually all states made clear to recipients that work was now seriously expected.[106]

The Effects of Reform. PRWORA exceeded the hopes of even its advocates. As intended, it sharply raised work levels among poor single mothers, both on and off welfare. Among mothers on the rolls, the share in work activities rose to a third, with about a quarter actually working.[107] More important, more poor mothers went directly to work rather than going on welfare at all. That raised work levels in the population. In 1993, only 44 percent of poor female heads of households with children worked at all, with only 9 percent full time and full year. By 1999 those figures jumped to 64 and 17 percent, respectively, before ebbing to 52 and 14 percent, respectively, by 2009.[108] Parallel to the work rates, poverty levels dropped both overall and for children, then rebounded somewhat.

Meanwhile, starting in 1994, the welfare caseload plummeted by around 70 percent through 2008, far more than anyone predicted. Millions of mothers simply left welfare for jobs. About 60 percent of the leavers went to work.[109] Although 40 percent did not, fears that they have suffered distress have not been substantiated. Some leavers were denied aid for failure to work, but states did not deliberately drive people off the rolls. Spending on cash aid shrank as caseloads collapsed, but federal and state governments spent even more money on the benefits necessary to move mothers into work—especially child care and the EITC. So overall spending on the poor rose. The main goal always was work, not to save money.

Reform also had clear limitations. It did not move all welfare mothers into work, and those who did take jobs were often still poor, although typically less so than they had been on welfare. Ideally, reform should be combined with additional measures to "make work pay." Reform did not reverse trends toward more unequal incomes, but it did slow them by raising earnings at the bottom of the society. Even with these limitations, welfare reform was the greatest victory government has won over working-aged poverty in forty years of struggle.[110]

PRWORA did not accomplish this alone. Superb economic conditions as well as the EITC and expanded child care helped to drive employment up and the rolls down. But of these forces, welfare reform was probably the most important.[111] This was what broke the mold of the old welfare and changed the signals heard by poor mothers. The new expectations were what caused many of them to bypass welfare and go directly to work.

A RECOVERY OF ORDER

Welfare reform paralleled other social policy successes in the 1990s. Some of the background causes of poverty abated. Although unwed childbearing overall continued to rise, childbearing among teens declined from 1991 to 2006–7 before turning back up. One reason might be that PRWORA placed more restraints on teen mothers, expecting them to live with parents and go to school. It gave a forceful message about personal responsibility.[112]

Crime also declined, after rising inexorably since the 1960s. The rate of violent crime soared from 161 offenses per 100,000 population in 1960 to 758 in 1991, before declining to 467 in 2007. The comparable figures for property crime were 1,726, 5,140, and 3,264. The gains came at a cost—imprisonment also soared; in 2008, 2.3 million Americans were behind bars in federal or state prison or in local jails.[113] But as I note below, improved programs to promote prison reentry also appeared

Although school reform has not yet yielded comparable progress, NCLB and parallel reforms at the state level have at least established the principle of accountability. It is already clear that if failing schools are seriously threatened with defunding or reorganization, they do perform better.[114] As NCLB is improved, this external pressure to improve will grow stronger and more effective.

All these trends reflect not only a society grown more conservative since the 1960s but also policies that deliberately enforced standards in these areas. The trends confirm that today's poverty is primarily a political and administrative problem rather than an economic one, as the label "poverty" might suggest. By improving its own institutions, government, backed by public opinion, can go far to restore order to poor areas. Then the spontaneous efforts of people to work and get ahead, largely in the private sector, can take over.

THE RESPONSE TO REFORM

The success of welfare reform and related policies called into question not only the way most experts had approached the poverty problem but also the critical perspectives I have described, both secular and religious. None of these viewpoints anticipated the combination of generosity and demands that characterized the new welfare regime. Far more prescient was the Bible's ancient vision of a restoration of community.

Expert Opposition. Most experts on poverty and welfare opposed reform in the shape it took. They too wanted to raise work levels among the poor, but they preferred to do so with voluntary methods that left work as a choice and did not enforce anything. But voluntary methods had failed, and the success of mandatory work programs gained a grudging recognition. Yet most experts continued to think of poverty as caused by economic and social barriers rather than weak expectations to work.

In this genteel world, the severe work demands embodied in PRWORA came as a shock. Most experts predicted disaster. Many welfare families would be unable to meet the new work requirements, they believed. They would simply be denied aid and thrown on the street.

To escape federal sanctions, states would compete to cut benefits and caseloads—a "race to the bottom." More than a million more children would be thrown into poverty.[115] After Clinton signed PRWORA, several experts resigned from his administration in protest. However, the effects of reform were overwhelmingly positive, and no "race to the bottom" occurred. Although caseloads fell as recipients went to work, states did not cut benefits—they actually raised them by strengthening work incentives, which allowed recipients to continue to draw some welfare at higher income levels.

Expert erred in part because PRWORA was instituted amid more favorable conditions than expected. In a worse economy or with less funding, results would surely have been less stunning. But two other factors were more important in explaining the experts' opposition. One was that the vast majority of researchers disapproved of this conservative brand of reform, especially PRWORA's candid willingness to enforce good behavior.

The other was the fact that most academic poverty experts are economists and sociologists. Most conduct their analyses entirely from behind their computers using data gathered by others. Those methods cannot gauge the institutional forces behind reform—the changes in policies and procedures that recast welfare, especially at the state and local level. Political leaders and administrators were the real heroes of reform, but even to perceive their role one must go out into the field and interview them. That is a low-tech form of research that commands little prestige in the university today. So academia missed the big story about reform—that the poor would respond to changed expectations once these were clear. The real barriers that sustain poverty are within politics rather than society or the economy.[116]

Secular Ideologies. Most secular critics of the old welfare system, including most advocates for the poor, had wanted welfare to be more generous. Above all, they affirmed its tradition of entitlement—paying aid without asking questions about "deservingness." That, however, was the principle that reform rejected above all else. Conservatives in Congress believed the old welfare had licensed lives of irresponsibility, and the public concurred. Aid was now to be based on reciprocity or conditionality: recipients had to earn their support by "doing the right thing."

Entitlement was tied to the idea of welfare as a safety net that would compensate for the insecurities of capitalism. To deny rights to aid, critics assumed, must mean to do less for the poor. Actually, work requirements were so popular that governments spent more on the reformed welfare system than they did on the old. Although it cost more, the new welfare was immensely more popular than the old precisely because it was work conditioned.

Libertarians who opposed welfare were also disappointed. They thought giving the poor money was inherently counterproductive. It meant paying a bounty on bad behavior—rewarding unwed mothers and runaway fathers. Welfare should simply be cut back. Charles Murray made that case forcefully before and during the welfare debates of the 1990s.[117] But the evidence that welfare actually created fatherless families was never strong. Most officials and voters believed that what was wrong with welfare was not aid per se but rather its permissive nature. To demand work of the dependent could make society's demands clear without foreclosing all assistance.

What emerged from reform was a new regime different from both the traditional liberal and conservative prescriptions. It was not a welfare state consisting only of rights and claims, a safety net against capitalism, as in the traditional social democratic vision. But neither was it a pure market system where the needy had to fend for themselves or expect aid only from private charity, as libertarians said. Welfare remained, but now it demanded the work effort that, in most cases, would keep families from needing assistance in the first place. It acquired a tutelary character. It reaffirmed rather than undercut the civilities of private society.

Church Opposition. In debates on welfare reform going back to the 1960s, religious voices had been the most permissive. In congressional hearings, Protestant and Catholic leaders alike called for more liberal benefits, and they fiercely resisted any idea of conditioning aid on work. After all, they reasoned, humans are created in the image of God, and God affirms the "dignity" of every individual, however poor in this life. Any attempt to enforce good conduct on the poor would violate that dignity. Rather, the needy should receive a larger share of America's bounty with no questions asked about lifestyle.[118]

But this reading denied the Bible's strictures about good behavior, going back to the Ten Commandments. Congress was not persuaded that the poor, however disadvantaged, should be exempted from the work expectations of the society. Polls showed that the Catholic hierarchy's protective view of the poor was not shared by most Catholics. Like most voters, the laity backed reform, supported the end of entitlement, and, on this question, refused to follow their religious leaders.[119] Then, the success of reform humbled church spokespersons, forcing more recognition of the value and possibility of work. Catholic statements have recently been less critical of reform than they were earlier.[120]

Like secular experts, however, the churches continue to think of poverty in terms of adverse social and economic forces. The goal of policy is still seen as liberating the poor from constraint by providing additional aid in various forms. Reform did have that aspect, as additional spending on support services was vital to its achievement. But at its core, reform *increased* constraint rather than reduced it. Recipients were obligated to work where previously they had not been, and most of the good effects of reform stemmed from this.

The churches fulfill that vision more nearly at the

local level than in Washington. Church institutions that serve the poor, such as Catholic parochial schools, do not hesitate to set standards and enforce good behavior, because this is necessary to their vision, even as their leaders tell Congress to spend more on the poor and downplay "deservingness." That official stance leads us away, rather than toward, the biblical vision of community.

Work requirements promoted social integration. The old welfare had largely been a separate world, holding its recipients apart from mainstream society. The new welfare, by enforcing work, threw recipients into much greater contact with the better off. In today's America, the workplace is the place where people most often meet others different from themselves. It is the center of American life, the main meaning that community has in our time. Thus, by raising work levels, reform moved America closer to the biblical vision of a single society.

5

THE WAY FORWARD

What should the nation and concerned citizens now do about poverty? Welfare reform shed considerable light on the nature of the problem and its solutions. And parallel to reform, other programs have appeared with a similar character. The best way forward is to complete welfare reform and expand these other directive programs. To that effort, religious believers and faith-based organizations can make an important contribution.

PATERNALISTIC PROGRAMS

Besides transforming welfare, the reform movement put a new form of social program on the map. The most effective reform programs, as in Wisconsin, not only linked welfare to work requirements but created special staffs to oversee recipients. These case managers were supposed to help recipients claim all the benefits they needed to work, such as child care, but they also checked up on them to be sure they worked or looked for work as they were supposed to do. In this they played a parental role, and programs with this close oversight came to be called paternalist.[121]

In several areas of antipoverty policy there is movement toward paternalism. Many programs to aid teen mothers, the homeless, school dropouts, or poor men have abandoned the permissive, value-free stance of the 1960s. They have become more directive, as it has become clear that their clients require this structure to live more effectively. All set clearer rules for client behavior and back them up with oversight. Evaluations confirm that paternalistic programs generally perform better than nondirective ones.

As one example, how to get children from disadvantaged backgrounds to learn in school has challenged education policymakers for decades. Ever since the 1960s, research has shown that merely to spend more on schools, as federal programs have done, achieves little. No Child Left Behind was the latest attempt to shake up federal aid so that schools would be more accountable for results. Subsidies were to be linked to performance obligations. In this broad sense, NCLB is analogous to TANF, although the onus to perform rests more directly on schools and teachers than on students.

Paternalism in education goes beyond this. The goals of schools are expanded from mere instruction to the direction of students' lives. In the most effective charter schools, principals and teachers set clear expectations for students, aim instruction at meeting them, test regularly for results, and provide individualized attention to students who lag. They also enforce good behavior more generally. Any inattention to teachers, and any conflict among students, distracts from learning. Such schools are poles apart from the more relaxed style favored by the education establishment, where teachers are much less directive and students are left freer to pursue their own impulses.[122]

Another example is work programs for poor men. A movement has arisen to establish what amounts to a work test for men who are already obligated to work.

That includes fathers who must work to pay child support judgments and ex-offenders leaving the prisons on parole, who are obligated to work in most states. Men from these groups who routinely fail to work are assigned to mandatory work programs. There their efforts to find and keep jobs are closely supervised. If they fail to cooperate, there are penalties, ultimately meaning to go to jail or back to prison. Evaluations of early programs like this are encouraging.[123]

Paternalistic programs confirm the insight that poor adults lack effective obligations more than opportunities or rights. Due to the disorganized families and communities around them, it seldom has been clear to them what they have to do to get ahead in life. The better off have usually faced much clearer expectations. These new, more directive programs help to close that gap.

FUTURE STEPS

America's best hope to reduce poverty is to complete welfare reform and continue to develop paternalistic programs in several areas of social policy.

Completing Welfare Reform. Despite the dramatic changes of the 1990s, the transformation of family welfare is still incomplete. The reform of 1996 left several loopholes by which states could avoid requiring welfare mothers to work. The reluctant states included California and New York, and because they had the largest caseloads, reform has not been fully implemented. The reauthorization of TANF in 2006 closed some of these loopholes, but others remain. Further improvements could be made at the next reauthorization, perhaps in 2011. On the other hand, Democrats in Congress may attempt to weaken existing work requirements. That would mean reducing the share of welfare mothers required to enter work activities and allowing more of them to go into education and training rather than work.[124]

Employment might also be better enforced in some other aid programs. Food stamps and housing programs already have work tests on the books, but they are weaker than in TANF's and not well implemented.

Paternalism. Paternalistic programs of the kind just described should also be expanded, both as part of welfare reform and beyond. Creating more schools of a highly directive character depends on allowing more charter schools within the public system and finding more principals and teachers willing and able to run them. They must expect ongoing resistance from the teacher colleges and unions.

Early children education programs like Head Start have not achieved much to date, but they might be improved with further experimentation and development. The need probably is for a more definite, more academic curriculum and better teachers. In both schools and preschool programs, merely to build up resources for the young will fail. Adding expectation to opportunity is far more important.[125]

Men's work programs should be cautiously expanded while more is learned about their effects and how best to design and implement them. More federal funding and evaluations can help. Ideally, for men, as for welfare mothers, better work tests should be combined with better work subsidies so that low-skilled men who work steadily have a better chance to support families. Consistent with the biblical vision, we should not hesitate to help the needy in practical ways, provided they also help themselves.[126]

Marriage. Currently, government has little mandate to tackle the marriage problem, because the public is far more tolerant of unwed pregnancy than nonwork. Government also has not yet developed programs able to impact the problem. Both difficulties may be easing. Since the liberated 1960s and 1970s, the culture has turned somewhat more conservative. A marriage movement has arisen that seeks to end no-fault divorce and change benefit programs to give some preference for married couples. Political support for pro-marriage policies, therefore, is rising.

The Bush administration funded local pro-marriage programs, and it began development of national programs that might be able to promote marriage. Mostly, these are counseling programs that teach couples, whether married or not, how to manage their conflicts so as to avoid breaking up. The programs, however, are entirely voluntary. They have had difficulty attracting and keeping participants, and the first evaluation results show scant effects.[127] If marriage once again becomes a norm among the poor, it will probably be due not to anything government does directly but to an impatient public opinion. Leaders high and low must simply convince low-income adults that they cannot achieve their goals without teamwork between spouses. And for enduring relationships, marriage is essential. Religious belief may also be essential, as traditionally this was the basis for marriage.[128]

FAITH-BASED CONTRIBUTIONS

This more paternalist social policy has emerged alongside a renewed interest by evangelicals in social problems, and this is not an accident. The new trend embodies a biblical approach to poverty that many churches and believers should naturally support.

The "religious right" arouses fear among many in Washington. The political class sees it as a force working to downsize government and terminate public concern for justice. Perhaps that was true ten or twenty years ago, but evangelicals recently have become less political and more concerned about improving their communities, including uplifting the poor.[129] The style of this movement is very different from the public crusades of the past. Rather than indict inequities and call for social change through government, it chiefly calls for more commitment by churches and individual Christians themselves. In short, it calls for community rather than redistribution.

The Bush administration called for greater involvement by "faith-based institutions" in the delivery of public programs for the poor. Welfare agencies had long contracted with nonprofit organizations to provide services such as child care and adoption. With welfare reform, contracting expanded, as private job placement agencies and other organizations were hired to promote jobs in welfare. The new work programs require many support services for clients, including child care, job placement, and postplacement follow-up. Faith-based programs are also prominent in recent efforts to help ex-offenders reenter society.

The new programs continue the tradition of church bodies working for public programs. The new movement, however, seeks greater legal rights for church agencies to hire staff that share their religious commitments—what is called "charitable choice"—rather than hire without reference to faith, as separation of church and state is often thought to require.

Volunteerism also must play a large role. Religious believers should support public policies in aid of the poor, but they should also have an individual mission to assist the poor in some specific way. That might mean helping out at a soup kitchen, tutoring a child in school, or mentoring a youth. In this, volunteers act out the biblical insight that to overcome poverty is more than an economic problem. It requires bringing the poor back into relationship. To achieve that, the needy must interact routinely with people better off than themselves—people who honor them with the same expectations as other people. Those relationships will not always be easy. Getting along with people who are different is the real labor of community. Volunteers can and must help do this work alongside the professional staffs.

Enforcing work or other civilities can appear severe, but the final purpose is acceptance. The poor are above all isolated, as poor in relationships as they are in resources. Work enforcement and paternalistic programs hope to reorganize lives to the point where the poor can undertake the standard relationships of the society—as workers, family members, and citizens. Only then do they truly come in from the cold. In that work, government must join hands with civil society.

6

LARGER QUESTIONS

Two larger questions can shed light on our struggle with poverty. One is how we should respond to poverty outside America. The other is how in general we should reason about poverty. On the first question, we are most aware of difference. Poverty in developing countries seems quite distinct from our own. Yet our best response turns out to be not unlike what we should do at home— offer help to poor countries, but also expect more efforts by them. On the second issue, we may expect sameness or continuity. Religious critics often mimic the prophets in criticizing our current efforts for the poor, as if nothing had changed since biblical times. But a great deal has changed both in the nature of poverty and in the capacities of government. So today a more modest stance is called for.

WORLD POVERTY

Destitution in much of the Third World is vastly worse than virtually anywhere in America. Confronted with that tragedy, some advocates for the poor, and some theologians, would extend our responsibility for poverty beyond our shores. Part of the argument is that rich countries such as the United States are in some way responsible for world poverty. If nothing else, we promoted the development of world capitalism, which has made poor countries dependent on the West, a view developed in liberation theology.[130] But after a century in which capitalism did vastly more to reduce world destitution than collectivism, that view is no longer defensible. Although the market economy involves insecurities for everyone, it has proved to be the friend of the poor, not their enemy.

The case also rests on a belief that, however world poverty arose, the United States and other rich countries can overcome it if we are generous. That view may sound convincing because the causes of world poverty are much more structural than with domestic poverty. In general, the poor abroad do not make themselves poor through family disarray or failure to work—they commonly work very hard. Rather, the economies of these countries are radically underdeveloped. Some argue, therefore, that transfers from rich countries such as America are the answer. Outside aid can allow desperate countries to invest in their economies, improve health conditions, and begin to grow steadily. The United Nations has set Millennium Development Goals to reduce the chief hardships of poor countries through Western aid.[131]

But the history of efforts to promote development in poor societies from outside is discouraging. Foreign aid, efforts to develop markets and trade, and even assistance toward better government—none has brought about lasting change. Some countries have gotten richer, notably in Asia, but that is due mostly to homegrown improvements in economies and government policies, not actions by the West. There is no one recipe for successful development.[132]

To ameliorate poverty abroad, just like at home, it appears that mutual effort is essential. Western aid can achieve something only if it supports efforts to improve things from within the aided countries. Unfortunately, in the developing world, such initiatives are weak.[133] The will to improve is often stronger outside these countries, among Western governments and nongovernmental organizations, than it is internally. Native elites are most concerned with preserving their own positions. They often oppose development because of the unwelcome social changes and political pressures it might bring. Even if there is economic growth, it may be controlled from above and not lead to democracy.[134]

A culture of defeat may not have produced dysfunctional patterns at the individual level in these countries, but it has at a collective level. Such is the resistance to change that people acquiesce in poverty or misrule. Many also struggle to emigrate to the West, but this is not a solution for the homelands they leave behind. Given the passivity of poor societies, there may simply be no way for the United States or its allies to save them, short of reasserting direct control of "failed states," as the UN has done in Haiti and parts of Africa.

This experience confirms the wisdom of Jesus's saying from the Sermon on the Mount: "Ask, and it will be given you; seek, and you will find; knock, and it will be opened to you."[135] Even a beneficent God cannot save people without their own participation. In Genesis, the Patriarchs not only ask, they also argue with God. That human beings are even allowed to ask for things from the higher powers is Good News that much of the non-West needs to hear. But asking is hard. Even to say what one wants is to assume some responsibility for one's life. For defeated cultures, this can be difficult to imagine.

The humanitarian impulse that says we should be responsible for world poverty must also be questioned. The Catholic bishops call for the United States to "empower people everywhere."[136] Some think that we are required by the Gospels to transfer much of our own wealth to poor countries.[137] But on the evidence, to do this would produce no lasting improvement. And it would deny the Good News to the rich. They would no longer be of value for themselves, but only as servants of the poor. That is a gospel of works that we must reject. God allows the better off to enjoy the bounty that he has given them—even if, mysteriously, it is more than others receive.[138]

Always, the biblical vision for a solution to poverty is rooted in community. We cannot be in community with billions of poor people on the other side of the world whom we never see or know personally. The call to exhaust our wealth for them is a call for sacrifice without relationship. Our obligation, rather, is toward the unfortunates we can see in and around our own lives. We need first, as Voltaire said, to cultivate our own garden.

FROM PROPHECY TO CHARITY

In the past, religious advocates for the poor have tended to adopt the prophetic voice. They imagine themselves, that is, "speaking truth to power" as the prophets do in the Old Testament. Both Catholic social teaching and the new social gospel promote this. But properly understood, the biblical tradition discourages grand claims about poverty or its solution. Two features mark the prophetic voice, and both should be questioned in our time.

Claims to Justice. First, the prophets and their latter-day followers speak in the language of justice. To claim justice means to specify rights and benefits that people should have simply as members of the community. Those who claim justice assert that they have been denied some established right, as the civil rights marchers did when they demonstrated against Jim Crow laws in the South. Claimants may also demand some new right or benefit that is not yet recognized, as does the current movement to allow homosexuals to marry or to serve openly in the military. As noted earlier, notions of the rights due to ordinary citizens have expanded over history, helping to build the welfare state. Seen with history's eye, further movement down this road can seem inevitable.

But claims to justice face demanding political tests. Supposed denials of rights must be proven, often in court. Those who claim new rights must convince the public and its representatives. Universal health care is an example of a right that was long claimed but only recently granted, in the 2010 national health legislation. Government also must be able to produce the redress that is sought. Not all human misfortunes, such as physical disabilities, can be turned into injustices that government can solve. Most fundamentally, to demand justice, claimants cannot assert only their own interests. They must make some appeal to the interests and values of other people as well.

The churches have often aligned themselves with movements seeking justice. Many clergy and seminary teachers supported all the progressive movement of the past century, including the union movement, feminism, and the current quest for gay rights. Clerical support for civil rights was particularly strong. That cause seemed especially fitted to the prophetic voice. Jim Crow was an abuse clearly contrary to American values, yet long ignored by the authorities.

But since the 1960s, claims to justice connected to poverty have faded. It has become much harder than it was in the 1960s or before to contend that poor people have been denied the essential rights of Americans. Nor—with the exception of health care—has it been easy to contend for rights to new social benefits. While advocates for the poor would like additional benefits often available in Europe, such as universal child care or guaranteed jobs, a majority of Americans and their leaders have not agreed. Most continue to think that the private economy covers most needs. Claims for the poor have taken on more and more the quality of complaint—asserting needs and injuries that, even if real, find little resonance in a broader public.[139]

The political problem is that the less privileged,

who would gain from new programs, are less "deserving" than they once were. Today's seriously poor are seldom like the jobless workers of the 1930s, idled by a massive economic breakdown. Most do not work steadily even when jobs are plentiful. Nor are they akin to the civil rights marchers, many of them college students who were well prepared to succeed once more equal opportunity opened. These same features also make the disadvantaged less able to protest on their own behalf. There is still considerable support for helping them, but it can no longer be *demanded* as a matter of *right*.

A Unilateral Voice. The other key feature of the prophetic voice is that it is unilateral. The prophets and those who emulate them do not engage in dialogue with their opponents. Rather, they speak entirely out of their own religious convictions. The judgments rain down from above upon the authorities, who do not reply. Or at least we do not hear their replies in the biblical texts.

This stance was fitting for a society where commitment to the poor was not yet established. One may doubt that Israel was ever so indifferent, given the concern for poverty seen in even the earliest Hebrew texts, but certainly not all of its rulers were attentive. The prophetic voice may also be warranted where government is undemocratic, as it was in most of the ancient world. Where the downtrodden lack channels to demand attention, charismatic outsiders such as the prophets may have to do so. In Jesus's time as well, Israel was a colony of

Rome. The conviction that government was remote and insensitive pervades both the Old and New Testaments.

But we live today thousands of years later. We know now that in biblical times the great age of political development was beginning. The Romans, though hated in Palestine, were the formative statesmen of the Western world. They proved that it was possible to govern a large territory on the basis of law and with serious attention to the public interest. Roman and also Greek politics had elected aspects. From the Middle Ages on, law-governed and responsive regimes developed in Europe, finally becoming the democratic states we see today. The British became the heirs of Rome, passing the rule of law and government by consent on to America and other colonies across the seas. The United States thus enjoyed from its founding the modern institutions that most countries still struggle to achieve.

Under such regimes, the prophetic voice is no longer appropriate. Modern governments have been schooled by the churches over centuries to care about the poor. They seldom need reminding of that duty today. There are still differences about how best to serve the poor or the public in general. But the gross self-serving and indifference spoken of by the Biblical prophets is not now our problem. Much more common is sincere disagreement about what serving the poor requires.

In this setting, religious advocates succeed best when they avoid trumpeting their convictions and instead honor the good intentions of others. They have influence because of their own effort and expertise. Rather than claim authority to judge opponents, they must work with others of different views. They must enter into the dialog about best policy that is central to democracy. This more modest stance is appropriate to the fortunate world we inhabit, where government might actually become—as it seldom seems in the Bible—an instrument of God's will.

> **RATHER THAN** *justice*, **THE PROPER RUBRIC**
> **FOR TODAY'S ANTIPOVERTY QUEST IS** *charity*.

Charity. Rather than justice, the proper rubric for today's antipoverty quest is charity. That is, we should be motivated to help the poor not because they have been denied some essential right but because God commands us to do so. Charity has a very different moral basis from justice. What defines it is not the consensus of the community about what is fair but rather what individuals think God calls them to do for the poor. The Good Samaritan rescues the man beaten by robbers not because his community expected this—indeed, it did not—but because of his personal compassion toward the victim.[140]

With charity, the political tests that justice imposes

are absent or relaxed. The poor need not have standing in their community. They need not be "deserving." Indeed, the Bible virtually defines them as the *un*deserving. We need not claim that they have been wronged. We need not identify with them, claiming that they are citizens just like the more privileged. We need not deny obvious differences between the poor and nonpoor. Rather, in the sight of God *everyone* is unworthy, poor and nonpoor alike. We also need not claim that helping them serves the interests of the nonpoor in any direct sense.

The poor might still have to prove their claims to those who help them, but the problem is reduced by the personal tie that charitable givers are supposed to have with those they aid. From that relationship, we are likely to know what people really need or not. On the other hand, claims cannot be contentious. In the world of charity, the needy do not make demands. Those who help them do not owe them anything. They are not expiating guilt. Their obligation is to God, not to those they aid. They are merely doing what they can to help people in need because God says to do so.

The tests for charity are moral. We must genuinely intend to help the poor and—most important—we must actually do so. Earnest intentions are not enough. The test is whether the poor actually do better, not whether we feel good about helping them. Indeed, helping today's poor often feels awkward just because it requires governing behavior. We cannot just give good things to needy people. As Max Weber wrote, policymakers must observe an ethics of "responsibility," not of "ultimate ends."[141]

Most recent initiatives in social policy reflect this turning from justice to charity. Over time, the debate over welfare reform in Congress turned away from heated arguments over what was fair to the poor toward more practical discussions about how best to manage the welfare system.[142] The replacement of AFDC by TANF signified, among other things, a shift from justice to charity as the main motivation behind welfare. That does not signify a diminution of commitment to the poor, as spending has risen. But the spirit behind helping has changed. Welfare is no longer seen as something the poor are owed as a matter of right. Rather, it represents our best effort at helping them. And it is always a work in progress.

ENDNOTES

1 Sar A. Levitan, Garth L. Mangum, Stephen L. Mangum, and Andrew M. Sum, *Programs in Aid of the Poor*, 8th ed. (Baltimore: Johns Hopkins University Press, 2003), 6.

2 U.S. Department of Commerce, Bureau of the Census, *Income, Poverty, and Health Insurance Coverage in the United States: 2009*, Series P-60, No. 238 (Washington, DC: U.S. Government Printing Office, September 2010), 4, 55.

3 Nicholas Eberstadt, *The Poverty of 'The Poverty Rate': Measure and Mismeasure of Want in Modern America* (Washington, DC: AEI Press, 2008).

4 Robert E. Rector, Kirk A. Johnson, and Sarah E. Youssef, "The Extent of Material Hardship and Poverty in the United States," *Review of Social Economy 57*, no. 3 (September 1999): 358–59.

5 Mark R. Rank and Thomas A. Hirschl, "Rags or Riches? Estimating the Probabilities of Poverty and Affluence across the Adult American Life Span," *Social Science Quarterly 82*, no. 4 (December 2001): 651–69.

6 Isabel V. Sawhill, "Poverty in the U.S.: Why Is It So Persistent?" *Journal of Economic Literature 26*, no. 3 (September 1988): 1081.

7 Greg J. Duncan, Richard D. Coe, Mary E. Corcoran, Martha S. Hill, Saul D. Hoffman, and James N. Morgan, *Years of Poverty, Years of Plenty: The Changing Fortunes of American Workers and Families* (Ann Arbor: University of Michigan, Institute for Social Research, 1984), tables 2.2 and 3.2.

8 Caseload data from U.S. Administration for Children and Families; U.S. Congress, House, Committee on Ways and Means, *2008 Green Book: Background Material, and Data on the Programs within the Jurisdiction of the Committee on Ways and Means* (Washington, DC: U.S. Government Printing Office, 2009), 7.38.

9 James L. Sundquist, "Has America Lost Its Social Conscience—And How Will It Get It Back?" *Political Science Quarterly* 101, no. 4 (1986): 513–33.

10 Arland Thornton and Linda Young-DeMarco, "Four Decades of Trends in Attitudes toward Family Issues in the United States: The 1960s through the 1990s," *Journal of Marriage and Family* 63, no. 4 (November 2001): 1009–37.

11 Martin Gilens, *Why Americans Hate Welfare: Race, Media, and the Politics of Antipoverty Policy* (Chicago: University of Chicago Press, 1999).

12 Steve Farkas, Jean Johnson, Will Friedman, and Ali Bers, *The Values We Live By: What Americans Want from Welfare Reform* (New York: Public Agenda Foundation, 1996), 31–34.

13 Howard Shuman, Charlotte Steeh, and Lawrence Bobo, *Racial Attitudes in America: Trends and Interpretation* (Cambridge, MA: Harvard University Press, 1985).

14 Shanto Iyengar, "Framing Responsibility for Political Issues: The Case of Poverty," *Political Behavior* 12, no. 1 (March 1990): 19–40; Anne Schneider and Helen Ingram, "Social Construction of Target Populations: Implications for Politics and Policy," *American Political Science Review* 87, no. 2 (June 1993): 334–47.

15 Joshua Guetzkow, "Beyond Deservingness: Congressional Discourse on Poverty, 1964–1996," *Annals of the American Academy of Political and Social Science* 629 (May 2010): 173–97.

16 U.S. Office of Management and Budget, *Budget of the United States Government, Fiscal Year 2012* (Washington, DC: U.S. Government Printing Office, 2011), 85, 165; *Annual Statistical Supplement 2009, Social Security Bulletin* (Washington, DC: Social Security Administration, February 2010), 11, 45.

17 Justin Bryan, "Individual Income Tax Returns, 2008," *Statistics of Income Bulletin* 30, no. 1 (Fall 2010): 13.

18 *Annual Statistical Supplement 2009*, 7.1; *Budget 2012*, 165.

19 *2008 Green Book*, 7.14.

20 Suzanne H. Woolsey, "Pied-Piper Politics and the Child-Care Debate," *Daedalus* 106, no. 2 (Spring 1977): 127–45.

21 Douglas J. Besharov and Douglas M. Call, "Income Transfers Alone Won't Eradicate Poverty," *Policy Studies Journal* 37, no. 4 (November 2009): 600–605.

22 "Social Expenditure," *OECD Factbook 2009* (Paris: Organisation for Economic Co-operation and Development, 2009), 222–23.

23 Christopher Howard, *The Hidden Welfare State: Tax Expenditures and Social Policy in the United States* (Princeton, NJ: Princeton University Press, 1997).

24 Irwin Garfinkel, Lee Rainwater, and Timothy M. Smeeding, "A Re-Examination of Welfare States and Inequality in Rich Nations: How In-Kind Transfers and Indirect Taxes Change the Story," *Journal of Policy Analysis and Management* 25, no. 4 (Fall 2006): 897–919.

25 Besharov and Call, "Income Transfers," 605–18.

26 Ivar Lødemel and Heather Trickey, *"An Offer You Can't Refuse": Workfare in International Perspective* (Bristol, UK: Policy Press, 2001).

27 Theda Skocpol, "Sustainable Social Policy: Fighting Poverty without Poverty Programs," *American Prospect* 1, no. 2 (Summer 1990: 58–70.

28 Gilens, *Why Americans Hate Welfare*, 42–45, 213–15.

29 U.S. Department of Commerce, Bureau of the Census, *Income, Poverty, and Health Insurance Coverage in the United States: 2009*, Series P-60, No. 238 (Washington, DC: U.S. Government Printing Office, September 2010), tables B-1, B-2.

30 Ron Haskins and Isabel Sawhill, *Creating an Opportunity Society* (Washington, DC: Brookings, 2009), 15–17, 203–4.

31 Lawrence M. Mead, *The New Politics of Poverty: The Nonworking Poor in America* (New York: Basic Books, 1992), 53–55.

32 U.S. Department of Health and Human Services, National Center for Health Statistics, *Health, United States, 2010* (Hyattsville, MD: National Center for Health Statistics, February 2011), table 7.

33 Quoted in Haskins and Sawhill, *Creating an Opportunity Society*, 208–10.

34 U.S. Department of Commerce, Bureau of the Census, Series P-60, No. 35, tables 3 and 13, and No. 68, table 8; Bureau of the Census, March 2009 Annual Social and Economic Supplement, table 14.

35 Harry J. Holzer, Paul Offner, and Elaine Sorensen, "Declining Employment among Young Black Less-Educated Men: The Role of Incarceration and Child Support," *Journal of Policy Analysis and Management* 24, no. 2 (Spring 2005): 330–33.

36 Samuel P. Huntington, *Who Are We? The Challenges to America's National Identity* (New York: Simon and Schuster, 2004), 69–75.

37 For ethnographic accounts of inner-city families, see Elijah Anderson, *Code of the Street: Decency, Violence, and the Moral Life of the Inner City* (New York: Norton, 1999); Leon Dash, *Rosa Lee: A Mother and Her Family in Urban America* (New York: Basic Books, 1996); and Jason DeParle, *American Dream: Three Women, Ten Kids, and the Nation's Drive to End Welfare* (New York: Viking, 2004).

38 The following section summarizes and updates Mead, *New Politics of Poverty*, chaps. 4–7.

39 Bureau of the Census, March 2010 Current Population Survey, table 22.

40 Gary Burtless, "The Work Response to a Guaranteed Income: A Survey of Experimental Evidence," in *Lessons from the Income Maintenance Experiments: Proceedings of a Conference Held in September 1986*, ed. Alicia H. Munnell (Boston: Federal Reserve Bank of Boston, n.d.), 22–52.

41 The New Hope Project in Milwaukee was one such experiment. See Johannes M. Bos, Aletha C. Huston, Robert C. Granger, Greg J. Duncan, Thomas W. Brock, and Vonnie C. McLoyd, *New Hope for People with Low Incomes: Two-Year Results of a Program to Reduce Poverty and Reform Welfare* (New York: Manpower Demonstration Research Corporation, August 1999).

42 Holzer, Offner, and Sorensen, "Declining Employment," 330–33.

43 William Julius Wilson, *The Truly Disadvantaged: The Inner City, the Underclass, and Public Policy* (Chicago: University of Chicago Press, 1987); William Julius Wilson, *When Work Disappears: The World of the New Urban Poor* (New York: Knopf, 1996).

44 Lawrence M. Mead, "The Poverty Puzzle," *New York Post*, Sept. 20, 2010, 27.

45 I heard these opinions during interviews in six states in 2008–9 in the course of research for Lawrence M. Mead, *Expanding Work Programs for Men* (Washington, DC: AEI Press).

46 Gayle Hamilton, Stephen Freedman, and Sharon M. McGruder, *National Evaluation of Welfare-to-Work Strategies: Do Mandatory Welfare-to-Work Programs Affect the Well-Being of Children? A Synthesis of Child Research Conducted as Part of the National Evaluation of Welfare-to-Work Strategies* (Washington, DC: U.S. Department of Health and Human Services and U.S. Department of Education, June 2000).

47 Amalia R. Miller and Lei Zhang, "The Effects of Welfare Reform on the Academic Performance of Children in Low-Income Households," *Journal of Policy Analysis and Management* 28, no. 4 (Fall 2009): 577–99; Deborah Lowe Vandell and Janaki Ramanan, "Effects of Early and Recent Maternal Employment on Children from Low-Income Families," *Child Development* 63 (1992): 938–49.

48 U.S. Department of Commerce, Bureau of the Census, *Who's Minding the Kids: Child Care Arrangements, Summer 2006* (Washington, DC: Bureau of the Census), tables 1B and 6.

49 Maria Cancian and Sheldon Danziger, "Changing Poverty and Changing Antipoverty Policies," in *Changing Poverty, Changing Policies*, ed. Maria Cancian and Sheldon Danziger (New York: Russell Sage Foundation, 2009), 25.

50 Lisa A. Gennetian, Danielle A. Crosby, Aletha C. Huston, and Edward D. Lowe, "Can Child Care Assistance in Welfare and Employment Programs Support the Employment of Low-Income Families? *Journal of Policy Analysis and Management* 23, no. 4 (Fall 2004): 723–43.

51 Recently, some states have cut child care subsidies due to the recession. But this affects only the minority of mothers who are off welfare and have to pay for care. Child care is still assured to mothers on welfare. See Peter S. Goodman, "Cuts to Child Care Subsidy Thwart More Job Seekers," *New York Times*, May 24, 2010, A1, A16.

52 Harry J. Holzer and Michael A. Stoll, "What Happens When Welfare Recipients Are Hired?" (Washington, DC: Georgetown University, May 2000).

53 Bureau of the Census, *March 2008 Current Population Surveys for March 2008 and March 2010*, table 24.

54 Haskins and Sawhill, *Creating an Opportunity Society*, 209–10.

55 Andrew Cherlin and W. Bradford Wilcox, "The Generation That Can't Move Up," *Wall Street Journal*, September 2, 2010; Pamela Smock, Wendy D. Manning, and Meredith Porter, "'Everything's There Except Money': How Money Shapes Decisions to Marry among Cohabiters," *Journal of Marriage and Family* 67, no. 3 (August 2005): 680–96.

56 Edward Shils, "Plenitude and Scarcity," *Encounter*, May 1969, 37–57.

57 Kathryn Edin and Maria Kefalas, *Promises I Can Keep: Why Poor Women Put Motherhood before Marriage* (Berkeley: University of California Press, 2005)

58 Elijah Anderson, "The Story of John Turner," *Public Interest*, no. 108 (Summer 1992): 3–34.

59 William Ryan, *Blaming the Victim* (New York: Pantheon, 1971).

60 Lawrence M. Mead, *Beyond Entitlement: The Social Obligations of Citizenship* (New York: Free Press, 1986), chap. 3.

61 Michael Harrington, *The Other America: Poverty in the United States*, rev. ed. (Baltimore: Penguin Books, 1971).

62 Mead, *New Politics of Poverty*, chap. 2.

63 T. H. Marshall, "Citizenship and Social Class," in *Class, Citizenship, and Social Development: Essays by T.H. Marshall*, ed. T. H. Marshall (Garden City, NY: Doubleday, 1964), chap. 4; Carole Pateman, "Another Way Forward: Welfare, Social Reproduction, and a Basic Income," in *Welfare Reform and Political Theory*, ed. Lawrence M. Mead and Christopher Beem (New York: Russell Sage Foundation, 2005), chapter 2.

64 David Schmidtz and Robert E. Goodin, *Social Welfare and Individual Responsibility* (Cambridge: Cambridge University Press, 1998).

65 Charles Murray, *Losing Ground: American Social Policy, 1950–1980* (New York: Basic Books, 1984).

66 I confine myself here to Jewish and Christian traditions. Islam, however, also emphasizes charity to the poor. Biblical quotations come from the Revised Standard Version.

67 The following is based on John D. Mason, "Biblical Teaching and Assisting the Poor," *Transformation* 4, no. 2 (April 1987): 1–14.

68 Amos 5:21–24.

69 Matt. 23:23–24.

70 Matt. 6:2–4; Mark 14:5–7; John 12:8.

71 Matt. 8:2–3, 9:27–31, 15:22–28, 17:14–18, 20:29–34; Mark 1:40–42, 10:46–52; Luke 5:12–13, 17:12–14, 18:35–43.

72 He reacts this way to the man at the Pool of Bethesda, who does not answer his question (John 5:6–8), and to the woman with an issue of blood, who tried to be cured by touching his robe without facing him directly (Mark 5:25–33; Luke 8:43–47). The same impatience does not appear in Matt. 9:20–22.

73 Matt. 9:2, 27–30, 15:28; Mark 5:34, 10:52; Luke 7:50, 17:19.

74 Gustavo Gutiérrez, *A Theology of Liberation: History, Politics and Salvation*, trans. and ed. Caridad Inda and John Eagleson (Maryknoll, NY: Orbis Books, 1985).

75 John R. Schneider, *The Good of Affluence: Seeking God in a Culture of Wealth* (Grand Rapids, MI: Eerdmans, 2002), 123–27.

76 Lev. 19:15.

77 Matt. 8:4, 9:30, 12:16; Mark 1:43–44, 5:19, 43, 7:36, 8:26; Luke 5:14, 8:56; John 5:14, 8:11, 9:7.

78 Matt. 9:2–6; Mark 2:3–11; Luke 5:18–25; John 5:14, 8:11.

79 John 5:2–15.

80 *The Book of Common Prayer* (New York: Seabury Press, 1979), 57.

81 Matt. 4: 4; Ephesians 4:13.

82 Matt. 18:22.

83 Matt. 5:17–20, 12:48–50; Mark 3:31–35; Luke 8:19–21, 11:27–28, 16:16–17.

84 Matt. 7:12, 22:36–40; Mark 10:19, 12:29–31; Luke 10:25–28.

85 Dietrich Bonhoeffer, *The Cost of Discipleship* (New York: Macmillan, 1963), chap. 1.

86 Gen. 3:17–19; John 5:17.

87 Acts 20:34; I Cor. 4:12; Eph. 4:28, I Thess. 4:11; 2 Thess. 3:7–12.

88 Marvin Olasky, *The Tragedy of American Compassion* (Wheaton, IL: Crossway Books, 1992).

89 Leo XIII, *Encyclical Letter Rerum Novarum* (On the Condition of the Working Classes) (Rome: Vatican City, May 15, 1891); John Paul II, *Encyclical Letter Laborem Exercens* (On Human Work) (Rome: Vatican City, September 14, 1981); John Paul II, *Encyclical Letter Centesimus Annus* (On the Hundredth Anniversary of *Rerum Novarum*) (Rome: Vatican City, May 1, 1991).

90 National Conference of Catholic Bishops, *Economic Justice for All: Pastoral Letter on Catholic Social Teaching and the U.S. Economy* (Washington, DC: National Conference of Catholic Conference, 1986), secs. 170–215.

91 Ibid., sec. 193.

92 Ibid., secs. 38, 49.

93 Walter Rauschenbusch, *Christianity and the Social Crisis*, ed. Robert D. Cross (New York: Harper and Row, 1964).

94 Jim Wallis, *God's Politics: Why the Right Gets It Wrong and the Left Doesn't Get It* (San Francisco: HarperCollins, 2005).

95 Matt. 25:31–46.

96 Quoted in Wallis, *God's Politics*, 16.

97 Ronald J. Sider, *Rich Christians in an Age of Hunger: Moving from Affluence to Generosity* (Nashville, TN: W Publishing, 1997), xiv.

98 Nicholas Wolterstorff, *Until Justice and Peace Embrace: The Kuyper Lectures for 1981 Delivered at the Free University of Amsterdam* (Grand Rapids, MI: Eerdmans, 1983), 81–85.

99 Wallis, *God's Politics*, 6, 48, 227; Wolterstorff, *Until Justice and Peace Embrace*, 81.

100 U.S. Congress, House, Committee on Ways and Means, *Overview of Entitlement Programs: 1990 Green Book: Background Material and Data on Programs within the Jurisdiction of the Committee on Ways and Means* (Washington, DC: U.S. Government Printing Office, June 5, 1990), 580.

101 Barbara Goldman, Daniel Friedlander, and David Long, *Final Report on the San Diego Job Search and Work Experience Demonstration* (New York: Manpower Demonstration Research Corporation, February 1986); Gayle Hamilton and Daniel Friedlander, *Final Report on the Saturation Work Initiative Model in San Diego* (New York: Manpower Demonstration Research Corporation, November 1989).

102 James Riccio, Daniel Friedlander, and Stephen Freedman, *GAIN: Benefits, Costs, and Three-Year Impacts of a Welfare-to-Work Program* (New York: Manpower Demonstration Research Corporation, September 1994); Gayle Hamilton, Stephen Freedman, Lisa Gennetian, Charles Michalopoulos, Johanna Walter, Diana Adams-Ciardullo, Anna Gassman-Pines, Sharon McGroder, Martha Zaslow, Surjeet Ahluwalia, Jennifer Brooks, Electra Small, and Bryan Ricchetti, *National Evaluation of Welfare-to-Work Strategies: How Effective Are Different Welfare-to-Work Approaches? Five-Year Adult and Child Impacts for Eleven Programs* (New York: Manpower Demonstration Research Corporation, November 2001).

103 Lawrence M. Mead, "Expectations and Welfare Work: WIN in New York State," *Polity* 18, no. 2 (Winter 1985): 224–52; Lawrence M. Mead, "The Potential for Work Enforcement: A Study of WIN," *Journal of Policy Analysis and Management* 7, no. 2 (Winter 1988): 264–88; Lawrence M. Mead, "Optimizing JOBS: Evaluation versus Administration," *Public Administration Review* 57, no. 2 (March/April 1997): 113–23.

104 Lawrence M. Mead, "The Politics of Conservative Welfare Reform," in *The New World of Welfare: An Agenda for Reauthorization and Beyond*, ed. Rebecca M. Blank and Ron Haskins (Washington, DC: Brookings Institution, 2001), chap. 7.

105 Lawrence M. Mead, "State Political Culture and Welfare Reform," *Policy Studies Journal* 32, no. 2 (May 2004): 271–96.

106 Thomas L. Gais, Richard P. Nathan, Irene Lurie, and Thomas Kaplan, "Implementation of the Personal Responsibility Act of 1996," in *New World of Welfare*, chap. 2

107 Data from the U.S. Administration for Children and Families; U.S. Congress, House, Committee on Ways and Means, *2004 Green Book: Background Material, and Data on the Programs within the Jurisdiction of the Committee on Ways and Means* (Washington, DC: U.S. Government Printing Office, March 2004), 7.81.

108 Data from the Bureau of the Census, *March Current Population Survey* for 1994 (table 19), 2000 (table 17), and 2010 (table 15).

109 Gregory Acs, Pamela Loprest, and Tracy Roberts, "Final Synthesis Report of Findings from ASPOE 'Leavers' Grants" (Washington, DC: Urban Institute, November 27, 2001).

110 For a comprehensive assessment see Blank and Haskins, *New World of Welfare*, and Richard P. Nathan, ed., "Welfare Reform after Ten Years: Strengths and Weaknesses," *Journal of Policy Analysis and Management* 26, no. 2 (Spring 2007): 369–85.

111 Jeffrey Grogger, "Welfare Transitions in the 1990s: The Economy, Welfare Policy, and the EITC," *Journal of Policy Analysis and Management* 23, no. 4 (Fall 2004): 671–95.

112 Haskins and Sawhill, *Creating an Opportunity Society*, 210–18.

113 Crime rate data from U.S. Department of Justice, Bureau of Justice Statistics; Heather C. West and William J. Sabol, "Prison Inmates at Midyear 2008—Statistical Tables," U.S. Department of Justice, Bureau of Justice Statistics, March 2009, table 15.

114 Eric A. Hanushek and Margaret E. Raymond, "Does School Accountability Lead to Improved Student Performance?" *Journal of Policy Analysis and Management* 24, no. 2 (Spring 2005): 297–327.

115 Ron Haskins, *Work over Welfare: The Inside Story of the 1996 Welfare Reform Law* (Washington, DC: Brookings, 2006), 288–96.

116 Lawrence M. Mead, "Research and Welfare Reform," *Review of Policy Research* 22, no. 3 (May 2005): 401–21; Lawrence M. Mead, "Policy Research: The Field Dimension," *Policy Studies Journal* 33, no. 4 (November 2005): 535–57.

117 Murray, *Losing Ground*; Charles Murray, "The Coming White Underclass," *Wall Street Journal*, October 29, 1993, A14.

118 Mead, *Beyond Entitlement*, 212–15.

119 Mary Jo Bane, "Personal Responsibility Means Social Responsibility," in *Lifting Up the Poor: A Dialogue on Religion, Poverty and Welfare Reform*, ed. Mary Jo Bane and Lawrence M. Mead (Washington, DC: Brookings Institution Press, 2003), 148–51.

120 National Conference of Catholic Bishops, *A Decade after Economic Justice for All: Continuing Principles, Changing Context, New Challenges* (Washington, DC: National Conference of Catholic Bishops, 1995); Thomas J. Massaro, *United States Welfare Policy: A Catholic Response* (Washington, DC: Georgetown University Press, 2007).

121 The following is based on Lawrence M. Mead, ed., *The New Paternalism: Supervisory Approaches to Poverty* (Washington, DC: Brookings, 1997), and Lawrence M. Mead, *Government Matters: Welfare Reform in Wisconsin* (Princeton, NJ: Princeton University Press, 2004), chap. 8.

122 David Whitman, *Sweating the Small Stuff: Inner-City Schools and the New Paternalism* (Washington, DC: Thomas B. Fordham Institute, 2008).

123 Lawrence M. Mead, *Expanding Work Programs for Poor Men* (Washington, DC: AEI Press, 2011), chaps. 1–7.

124 Lawrence M. Mead, "Work versus Education and Training in TANF," hearing on "The Role of Education and Training in the Temporary Assistance for Needy Families (TANF) Program," Subcommittee on Income Security and Family Support, Committee on Ways and Means, U.S. House of Representatives, 111th Cong., 2nd sess., April 22, 2010.

125 The much-noted Harlem Children's Zone, for example, tried initially merely to build up services for poor children, but it found that for children to succeed in school it was necessary to be more demanding. See Paul Tough, *Whatever It Takes: Geoffrey Canada's Quest to Change Harlem and America* (Boston: Houghton Mifflin, 2008).

126 Mead, *Expanding Work Programs for Men*, chaps. 8–9.

127 Robert G. Wood, Sheena McConnell, Quinn Moore, Andrew Clarkwest, and JoAnn Hsueh, *Strengthening Unmarried Parents' Relationships: The Early Impacts of Building Strong Families* (Princeton: Mathematic Policy Research, May 2010).

128 Lawrence M. Mead, "Social Policy and Marriage," in *Handbook of Families and Poverty*, ed. D. Russell Crane and Tim B. Heaton (Thousand Oaks, CA: Sage, 2007), chap. 2.

129 David D. Kirkpatrick, "The Evangelical Crackup," *New York Times Magazine*, October 28, 2007.

130 Gutiérrez, *Theology of Liberation*.

131 Jeffrey Sachs, *The End of Poverty: Economic Possibilities for Our Time* (New York: Penguin, 2005)

132 William Easterly, *The White Man's Burden: Why the West's Efforts to Aid the Rest Have Done So Much Ill and So Little Good* (New York: Penguin Books, 2007).

133 Francis Fukuyama, *State-Building: Governance and World Order in the 21st Century* (Ithaca, NY: Cornell University Press, 2004), chap. 1.

134 Bruce Bueno de Mesquita and George W. Downs, "Development and Democracy," *Foreign Affairs* 84, no. 4 (Sept.–Oct. 2005): 77–86.

135 Matt. 7:7.

136 National Conference of Catholic Bishops, *Economic Justice for All*, sec. 292.

137 Sider, *Rich Christians in an Age of Hunger*.

138 John R. Schneider, *Good of Affluence*, 87–89.

139 Lawrence M. Mead, "Is Complaint a Moral Argument?" in *NOMOS XLIV: Child, Family, and State*, ed. Stephen Macedo and Iris Marion Young (New York: New York University Press, 2003), chap. 4

140 Luke 10:29–37.

141 Max Weber, "Politics as a Vocation," in Max Weber, *From Max Weber: Essays in Sociology*, ed. and trans. H. H. Gerth and C. Wright Mills (New York: Oxford University Press, 1958), chap. 4.

142 Lawrence M. Mead, "Welfare Politics in Congress," *PS: Political Science and Politics* 44, no. 2 (April 2011): 345–56.

ABOUT THE AUTHOR

Lawrence M. Mead is a visiting scholar at the American Enterprise Institute and professor of Politics and Public Policy at New York University. He has been a visiting professor at Harvard, Princeton, and the University of Wisconsin and a visiting fellow at Princeton and at the Hoover Institution at Stanford. Professor Mead is an expert on the problems of poverty and welfare in the United States. Among academics, he was the principal exponent of work requirements in welfare, the approach that now dominates national policy. He is also a leading scholar of the politics and implementation of welfare reform and work programs for men. His many books and articles on these subjects have helped shape social policy in the United States and abroad.